THE LOIRE

Seán Jennett

THE LOIRE

with 36 photographs by the author

B. T. Batsford Ltd. *London and Sydney*
Hastings House Publishers *New York 10016*

First published 1975
© Seán Jennett 1975

Made and printed in Great Britain by
Richard Clay (The Chaucer Press), Ltd, Bungay, Suffolk
for the publishers B. T. Batsford Ltd
4 Fitzhardinge Street, London W1
and 23 Cross Street, Brookvale, NSW 2100, Australia

ISBN 0 7134 2974 7

Library of Congress Cataloging in Publication Data

Jennett, Seán.
  The Loire.

   1. Loire Valley—Description and travel. I. Title.
DC611.L81J46 1975   914.4'5   74–22428
ISBN 0–8038–4293–7

Contents

Illustrations

Acknowledgements

I am grateful for assistance received in the preparation of this book from the London and Paris offices of the French Government Tourist Office and from the following:

Monsieur Michel Hollande, Délégué régional au Tourisme, Préfecture, 45 Orléans.

Monsieur P. J. Levèque, Délégué départemental au Tourisme, Préfecture, 37 Tours.

Monsieur Marc Ribaud, Directeur, Comité Départemental de Tourisme, Cité Administrative, 49008, Angers.

Visitors who require information may obtain it from these addresses.

The stanza on page 50 from 'When you are old and grey' by W. B. Yeats is quoted from *The Collected Poems of W. B. Yeats* by permission of M. B. Yeats, Miss Anne Yeats, Macmillan of London and Basingstoke, and Macmillan Company of Canada.

I owe especial thanks to my wife Irene, who kept my records while on tour in the Loire valley, filed and classified information, and finally typed the book for publication.

Introduction

Nearly every book about the Loire begins by saying that the river is the longest in France, and this is true. The valley of the Loire therefore rightly extends from the source of the river 4,500 feet up on the Gerbier de Jonc in the Massif Central down to the point where it meets the sea at Saint-Nazaire. Yet this is not what is commonly meant when the valley of the Loire is in question. The popular definition of the term is that part of the river made notable by the presence of a series of splendid royal and noble châteaux along its course. Where this begins and where it ends is not a matter for exact statement and it is necessary in a book such as this to make an arbitrary choice, for there are châteaux of one sort or another everywhere along the river or in its confluent valleys. For the purpose of this book the valley of the Loire begins at Gien, because this was a royal château, and it ends at Angers, because here was another.

This length of the Loire, some 150 miles, has a number of tributaries. From the south come the Cher, the Indre, the Vienne, and the Thouet, and from the north the little river Cisse, near Blois, and the Maine, the latter the conjunction of the Mayenne, the Sarthe, and the Loir—the last of these, be it noted to avoid confusion, being masculine and e-less, to distinguish it from the feminine Loire.

The Loire may be the longest river in France, but it is also one of the most useless, in the commercial sense. It has been navigable, in the past, by flat-bottomed boats that went down

with the current and returned with great difficulty and expenditure of labour and of time—so much so that certain types
of boats were made for one downstream trip only, to be broken
up at the end of the journey. There is no navigation on the
river between Gien and Angers today. The river is shallow and
encumbered with sandy islands. These islands, with their yellow margins, green osiers, and young trees, may be hindrances
from the point of view of utility, but they are also very beautiful
accessories of the Loire. Some of them have, too, a quality of
impermanence. Almost anything may be the birth of an island—
a dead branch that anchors itself on the bed forms an obstruc-
tion against which sand builds up, and lo! in a month or two a
new island is born. It may die in the winter, however. The cold
season brings a rush of water and fearsome floods that would
spread over the surrounding countryside if they were allowed.
They are prevented by the corsets and straitjackets of miles
of embankments. Along the summits of these, in some places,
roads or footpaths run, with marvellous views of the river. On
the other hand, in the summer the water dwindles until only a
sparse stream flows among the sandy islands and islets.

The valley of the Loire as we have defined it lies for the larger
part in carboniferous strata of a soft white stone called in French
tuffeau, which for miles rises as low cliffs. The stone is so easily
cut that the inhabitants of the valley have made houses by
excavating rooms in the cliff face, indeed, whole suites of
rooms. These are squared off and have doors and windows and
are provided with fireplaces and all modern services, so that
you would never know that you were not in an ordinary house.
It is curious, as you climb paths up the cliff, to find a smoking
chimney by your feet, or round a bend of the path to come upon
one or a group of these dwellings set high above the river. You
will find such dwellings, some now turned into workshops or
store-rooms, along miles of the Loire, notably at Vouvray;
or beside the Loir at Troo. Those who live in masonry houses
affect to despise the cave-dwellers, whom they call troglodytes;
the troglodytes prefer their cliff houses, which have the merit of

maintaining an equable temperature in the cold of winter as in the heat of summer.

If we were to count the valley of the Loire as including those of its tributaries between Gien and Angers, we should still have a subject too vast for a book of this size. I do not know how many châteaux there may be in this area, but certainly it must be near, perhaps over, four hundred, to say nothing of churches, cathedrals, monasteries, and so on, in all of which categories there is very much of interest to be visited and enjoyed in the valley of the Loire. So this book is selective. I make no apology for having neglected this or that place, though it may be your favourite, which you feel passionately ought to be a star in any book on the Loire. A book, or more than one book, may be written on out-of-the-way places in that valley, but this is not it; this book intends to take you by the hand along ways that may be well worn, but nevertheless retain interest and charm.

We shall pass through the territories of three ancient provinces, of Orléans, of Touraine, and of Anjou, strung along the blue river. The Orléanais includes the district of Sologne, to the south of the great bend between Gien and Chambord, where the Loire, which has so far flowed south to north, finally turns westward. Sologne is wooded country, so profusely scattered with little lakes that one might suppose some vast giant to have stepped here upon a fragment of glass, crushing it beneath his heel and scattering bits and slivers in every direction. North of the river is the Beauce, largely wheat country. Touraine includes the Blésois, the district around Blois. Anjou is one of the cradles of the English monarchy, for from Angers came the Angevin or Plantagenet dynasty, which ruled more of France than did the King of France himself and supplied more kings to occupy the English throne that has any other dynasty before or since.

1. How the Châteaux came about

What is a château? What is this object, this kind of building that
has become so notable in the Loire valley? We have no word in
English that is exactly the equivalent of the word 'château'.
Even the French are uncertain of the extent of its meaning.
Larousse defines it as a *demeure féodale fortifiée*, but this, though it
covers adequately such buildings as Chinon, Loches, Plessis-
Bourré, and Langeais, will not do for such as Cheverny,
Montgeoffroy, and Valençay, and many others, which plainly
are not fortified.

The word 'château' has the same origin as the English 'castle',
from Latin *castellum*. With few exceptions, and those somewhat
self-conscious (Castle Howard, for instance), English 'castle'
means a fortified building, of medieval origin, or even something older but still clearly defensive (Maiden Castle). If one
cannot imagine an earthwork being called a 'château', the
word is nevertheless of wide significance, and might be arrived
at in English if one could combine 'castle' and 'stately home' and
'palace' into one embracing and somewhat indiscriminate
term. We should then have something that could be applied as
imprecisely as the word 'château' to the grim medieval fortress of Angers, the more civilised castle of Plessis-Bourré, the
great palaces of Blois and Chambord, and the country house
of Montgeoffroy.

Many of the châteaux began as castles or fortresses pure and
simple. They were the headquarters or sub-quarters of warring
barons constantly seeking to extend their rule over various pieces

of territory, barons of whom the exemplar is the ferocious and notorious Foulques Nerra, the Black Falcon. In a life of constant aggression and castle-building Foulques laid his hand, from his centre at Angers, on much of Touraine and Berry. When he momentarily grew tired of bloodshed and rapine he would purge his soul by going on a pilgrimage, and then, refreshed and purified, carry on as before.

There are châteaux everywhere in France, founded in the baronial struggles of the middle ages. These disturbances were at times directed against the king, and succeeded in pushing the court out of Paris and into the Loire valley. It was the presence of the court in that valley that eventually brought fashion and invention to the district. If fashion and invention were expressed in mány ways that have left little trace or the results of which have vanished into museums, with the royal influence came a series of new modes of architecture expressed in châteaux. Many of these buildings have survived, more or less changed, neglected, or restored by succeeding generations. It is these that have made the Loire valley what it is for us today.

The influence of the court in the Loire valley began after the arrival of the young Dauphin Charles, son of Charles VI. He had left Paris in a hurry, gathered up in a dressing-gown in the arms of the Breton Tanguy du Châtel, as the Burgundians invaded the city. Though in due course he became Charles VII, Charles did not again enter Paris until twenty years had elapsed, and even then he soon returned to the country south of the Loire, where he had the castles of Chinon and Loches. It was at Chinon that Jeanne la Pucelle had come to him to persuade him to take up arms against the English and to be no longer merely the King of Bourges, as he was derisively called, but truly the King of France. Charles, who became Charles the Victorious, died at Méhun-sur-Yèvre, near Bourges, in 1461.

His successor Louis XI might have lived in Paris, but he chose to lead a nomadic existence, trailing his court from town to town, from province to province. Whenever he could he would come to the Loire valley, and eventually he retired to Tours, to the château of Plessis-lès-Tours.

Louis's son and successor, Charles VIII, was born at Amboise and spent his boyhood there. Amboise never lost its place in his affections, and when he came to the throne he determined to make it the greatest palace on the Loire, perhaps in France. An enormous building programme was set in train. This work was in full swing when Charles undertook an expedition to Italy to assert the claim of the French royal house to the kingdom of Naples. He conquered Naples readily, but met with violent objection from the whole of Italy and was forced to withdraw.

In Italy Charles saw something that both amazed and enlightened him and filled him with enthusiasm. It was the Renaissance. He saw it in gardens, in sculpture and ornament, and in buildings. Suddenly what he was putting up at Amboise, all that vast and ambitious project, seemed valueless and *démodé*. Charles determined to take the Renaissance back to France. He gathered a great collection of precious objects, which made loads for six thousand mules, and in company with these he assembled twenty-two learned men, architects, decorators, artists, and men of divers other skills, including one who knew how to breed chickens in incubators. This long, long train, probably going two by two, set out for France, and for the château of Amboise. It was a marvellous and tempting sight and it was ambushed at Fornova. Charles, it is said, won a victory, but he lost a great quantity of his goods. With the remainder and the twenty-two men he continued his journey.

Charles's learned and skilled men and Charles's caravan of fine objects were to have a great effect but Charles himself was not to see it. One day in 1498, at Amboise, he bent his head to pass through a low doorway, struck his forehead on a beam, and apparently suffered concussion. He complained of headache and dizziness, fell to the floor, and in a few hours he died.

Another branch of the royal family had its centre at Orléans and at Blois—particularly Blois. There, Charles, the young Duke of Orléans, amused himself by writing poetry—he was a genuine and accomplished poet whose work retains charm and readability today. He was altogether a more attractive person than most of his relations. When Henry v invaded France Charles readily gathered men at arms and joined the great army that was being assembled to oppose the English. With that army he suffered the disaster of Agincourt. Beneath one of the heaps of dead and wounded on that appalling battlefield the victorious English discovered Charles unhurt, trapped in his own heavy armour. For them he was the greatest prize of that day of great prizes. They carried him off to England and held him there for twenty-five years while he tried by correspondence to raise his enormous ransom.

When at last he returned to Blois he began to rebuild the château, which was then a medieval fortress, in a more comfortable and more domestic style in brick. The lowest of the four wings of the present courtyard is his work.

After his release Charles married for a third time and begot a son, who was to become Louis xii.

Louis xii in his turn began to rebuild Blois, in a rather more ambitious style than his father had followed, making of the château the premier residence of the crown and the court. France was ruled from Blois. Where the king was, courtiers came, as they had in the time of Charles viii, and looked for estates and sites on which to build their own châteaux. Great houses proliferated in the Loire valley and existing castles began to be altered and their stern discomfort ameliorated.

Louis was married to Jeanne, daughter of Louis xi, but it was a marriage he did not enjoy—Jeanne appears to have been no beauty—and he found small advantage in it. He had the marriage to Jeanne annulled and married Anne de Bretagne, who had been the wife of Charles viii and now for the second time became Queen of France. By this marriage Louis gained the largely independent duchy of Brittany, adjacent to the Loire valley and not far from his court at Blois. The elaborated initials of Louis and Anne are seen in several places in the château of Blois, together with Louis's emblem, the porcupine.

Louis's daughter Claude de France married her father's cousin François d'Angoulême. He was a tall and energetic young man apparently of considerable charm, despite the possession of an extravagant version of the long and thin Valois nose. With the extravagant nose went extravagant tastes. He was fond of sport, fond of hunting in the great woods and forests of Amboise, where he had been brought up under the careful eye of his mother Louise de Savoie, fond of the country-side, fond of women—he bought great quantities of expensive gowns for the ladies of his court; he was open-handed to excess, and he was joyous in the power of kingship (he succeeded his cousin in 1515). He too began to rebuild Blois, and he had largely completed one amazing wing when his queen Claude died. This loss may have been the cause of the cessation of work at Blois, but if it was not, then the disaster that followed certainly was. François determined to reclaim the duchy of Milan, which he had reason to regard as rightly his by inheritance. He suffered a defeat at Pavia and was captured. The next two years he spent in the hands of the Spaniards in Madrid. He appears to gave given thought during his captivity to what was best for France and he decided henceforward to live in the capital city, Paris. On regaining his freedom, he announced '*de dorénavant faire la plupart de sa demeure et séjour en sa bonne ville et cité de Paris et à l'entour*' (to dwell for the greater part in his good town and city of Paris and in the neighbourhood).

'*A l'entour*', in the neighbourhood, was to mean a new château, the château of Madrid, which was to be built in the Bois de Boulogne. The masons, the joiners, and the carvers who had been working at Blois were brought to Paris for this new work. Henceforward the Loire valley was no longer to be a dwelling-place of kings, no longer the centre of innovation, fashion, and style. Kings kept their châteaux and they came and visited, or stayed to hunt in the many rich forests, but they lived here no longer. The great château of Chambord rose among the trees and swamps, but in use it was no more than a gigantic hunting-lodge, to which the court came only occasionally, following

1. The château at Gien, of brick with patterned walls

2. Sully, a gothic fortress

3. Romanesque
   capital at
   Saint-Benoît

4. The monument
   to Louis XI at
   Cléry-Saint-
   André

after an army of servants who brought furniture and tapestries and got all ready in advance. The same servants dismantled everything after the court had gone. Royal favourites occupied some of the châteaux—Diane de Poitiers at Chenonceau and Chaumont, and much later Madame de Pompadour at Ménars. The queen-mother Catherine de Médicis came to Chenonceau perhaps as much to spite her rival Diane as for any other reason.

During all this time the meaning of a château, what it was, and the style of its use and of its building, was changing. Anyone may see that a château such as Chinon, such as Loches, such as Angers, is a grim place in which the walls that keep an enemy out also keep the dweller in. The intentionally difficult access made an undesirably difficult egress. As long as violence, raids, and wars, with their consequent sieges, might endure, no one was inclined to complain overmuch of the inconvenience of the defences.

A different conception came with Jean Bourré. One of the principles of Louis xi, ruling at the end of the Hundred Years War, in which the nobility had been such trouble for the Crown, was to employ men of the bourgeoisie in high office. Jean Bourré, who had been faithful to Louis in both troubled times and in good ones, was rewarded with the secretaryship of finance and control of the treasury of France. In this high office he became rich and built for himself the château of Plessis-Bourré, in a stretch of open, level country. There was here no salient mount or defensive site. Defence had necessarily to depend on moats. What was interesting about Plessis-Bourré was that, although defence must necessarily be regarded, the comfort, convenience, and pleasure of a house were important factors in the design. For this reason three of the wings round the courtyard were built lower than the fourth or principal wing, so that air and light might come in more freely and the closure might be less claustrophobic.

Louis was pleased with his treasurer's château and visited him occasionally, bringing all his court, with a huge number of staff, retainers, and servants, all of whom had to be fed by the host. Sometimes, during the king's stay, an embassy or two would arrive, with ambassadors, counsellors, secretaries, and others. Plessis-Bourré, the ideal of a fortified château, remains complete; it does not seem to have been large enough for such visitations of the locusts.

Jean Bourré had a hand in other châteaux, notably Langeais, built for the king. Langeais has the round towers with *poivrière* roofs that we see at Plessis-Bourré, furnished with machicolations both efficient and handsome, and with upper stages that are in retreat from the principal vertical. Bourré's influence went farther, to the large new château of Le Verger, now mostly destroyed, and to Bury, which is also almost completely gone.

You will see how Bourré's buildings and those that were influenced by him, though they may be strong and windowless on the lower floors, have large windows above through which light and air could be admitted to the interior. The château had become a house, with large rooms and chambers well ventilated and illuminated.

Some châteaux had gone further and in proportion as they rose from the ground became more and more elaborate. The windows became more numerous and more ornamented in the rich gothic manner, until above the battlements ornament proliferated into a crowd of fanciful chimneys, turrets, and pinnacles, all rich with colour and gold. Among these the roof itself, covered with lead, was gilt and gleaming. The whole thing was a delicate exercise in ornament set upon plain massive feet in a moat of water, in which the richness was redoubled. A supreme example of this kind of construction was the château of Saumur. It appears in a colourful illustration in the manuscript of the *Très Riches Heures du duc de Berry*. There it looks indeed like something from a fairy tale, a creation of the imagination, something altogether unbelievable, and all the more unbelievable in contrast with the massive and glum château Saumur is today. But it is true. There is every reason to believe that the illuminator of the *Très Riches Heures* was an exact and

accurate delineator. Where the existing château may be compared with the illustration the match is precise.

Saumur was not the only château with this glittering top-
hamper. There were others and there may have been many
others, for without illustrations parallel to those of the *Très
Riches Heures* we cannot know. We do know of Saumur and of
Méhun-sur-Yèvre. Yet the thing was impractical. Lightning
and the wind could knock off the pinnacles, and gunfire, as
guns became more efficient, would be fell in that forest of stone.
The desire for such a scintillating and intricate display could
survive several generations, however, for something of the kind
appeared again in the sixteenth century and survives for us to
see it today—the crowded, fantastic company of the roof of
Chambord.

After the return of Charles VIII from Italy, with his booty and
his clever men, the Renaissance began to appear in châteaux
newly built or newly altered or added to. It was for a time a
matter of appliqué work, of the addition of superficial ornament
in the new style, derived from Greece through the imperfect
digestion of Italy, and in France imperfectly understood.
Pilasters and pediments were enthusiastically adopted, with
much leafy, swirling ornament in bas-relief—bas-relief was itself a novelty, in contrast with the deeper carving of the gothic
style. The pointed arch of the medieval period gave way to the
square-headed opening for windows and doors, and windows
received crossed mullions and transoms. Arcades of round-
headed arches appeared, surmounted by string courses. Yet
beneath all this the plan remained persistently gothic. Symmetry in a façade was not required, doors, windows, towers, and
turrets were placed precisely where they were needed according
to criteria other than symmetry. And something else was kept.
Even where a château was completely rebuilt, the corner towers
and especially the tower or keep of the medieval castle were
retained. This may be seen notably at Chenonceau, where,
rewindowed and modernised, the old tower still stands, separate
from and in advance of the renaissance house. For the great

tower, the *donjon*, was the secure place where the deeds and charters of property owned by the lord of the château were kept —the muniment tower. The possession of such a tower was a sign and symbol of lordship, not to be lost by demolition.

Similarly battlements and machicolations were a symbol of lordship. As such they were controlled by licence from the king, both in England and in France. In 1520, when Bernard Salviati, a merchant, was given exceptional permission to fortify the château of Talcy with '*murs, tours, créneaux, barbacanes, canonières, machicoulis, pont-levis, boulevards*', in fact all the apparatus of a fortress, it was on the clear understanding that he should not, by reason of these fortifications, in any manner whatsoever entitle himself *seigneur châtelain*.

With the change of fashion the fortifications might disappear —even those licensed for Talcy seem never to have been built— but the great towers, the donjons, remained long afterwards, serving their two original purposes of storage of muniments and symbol of lordship. In both respects they attracted the enmity of the revolutionaries of 1789. In many châteaux the revolutionaries held bonfires of charters and other documents and so were responsible for considerable difficulty to future historians.

In parallel with the exterior, the interior of a château was changed by the Renaissance. The massive hooded fireplaces of the middle ages, the principal architectural ornament of a room, were retained in essence, but their decoration was converted to the new fashion. Ceilings of important chambers were plastered or coffered, the coffers being sometimes filled with paintings, as you may still see at Plessis-Bourré. The gross taste of the period might be reflected in these paintings, as it was also in carving, as on the front façade of the Louis xii wing at Blois. The most interesting development, however, was that of the staircase. The medieval staircase was a vice, a spiral contained in a vertical tube. It was never convenient, or even safe—who can say how many lords encumbered by cloaks and swords, how many ladies in their ponderous skirts, how many serving-men unable to see over their trays of dishes, tripped and fell

down those spiral stone stairs. Even where the steps are wide
and unusually shallow, as at Baugé and Montreuil-Bellay, the
inconvenience is not altogether removed, nor the meanness
much alleviated. For a better approach up the cliff to Amboise
Louis VIII built two great spiral ramps in the broad towers of the
Minimes and of Hurtault, so easy of ascent that a horseman
might ride up, as indeed horsemen did. At Blois François 1
retained the spiral stair, but enclosed it in an airy and elegant
open cage of masonry that became the principal feature of the
courtyard. He retained the spiral also at Chambord (plate 14)
but doubled it, a spiral within a spiral, in which one person
may go up and another come down without the two ever meeting. This also was built in an open stone cage, but set in the
centre of the great central block. It was not until later in the
Renaissance that it occurred to someone to take the staircase
up in a series of straight flights, from landing to landing; by
this plan the possibilities of design and the dignity of the staircase were increased.

The high Renaissance, with its luxury and richness of detail,
gave way to the classical period, the period of symmetry.
Whereas the organisation and purpose of a medieval and of a
renaissance house were reflected in and even dictated the exterior, that of a classical house had to be adapted to the all-
important symmetry of the façade. That façade was restrained
in ornament, at times even plain, though the interior might be
rich. The difference is fundamental, so much so that it seems to
require a different kind of mind to appreciate it. For one person
the classical style is inhuman, heartless, indifferent, in short
boring. Gothic and the Renaissance share a rumbustious liveliness, a delight in complexity and detail, that has vanished
from the classical. It depends on your point of view. The classical
châteaux such as Ménars, Cheverny, Serrant attract their
devotees.

Not all the interesting houses of the Loire are châteaux. There
are a number of smaller houses that are in some instances

between manors and châteaux, such as Villesavin and Fougères (plate 9), and smaller ones still that are simply farms. Some go by the delightful term of *gentilhommières*. René of Anjou, the good king René, who wrote poems and painted pictures and imagined himself King of Sicily and King of Jerusalem, grew tired of his great châteaux such as Angers and built for himself a number of smaller houses—still large enough for a considerable staff and for guests—one near each of his château. To these he would retire to write, to paint, to hear music, to hunt in the neighbouring woods, or to fish in a pond or lake that was the reason for the siting of the house. These small manors became popular and a number of them appeared in other parts of the Loire valley. Beauregard is one of the most interesting.

Among the benefits of the Renaissance was the invention of the pleasure garden. Charles VIII saw fine and beautiful gardens in Italy and as a consequence of his illumination there the fashion spread to France. In future every château had to have its garden and the gardener became a man of importance, of skill and stature. He had to be proficient in the use of tee-square and set square, in geometrical drawing, in order to plan terraces, parterres, arbours, ponds, fountains, and so on. The garden became the frame, the surround in which the château rose, a renaissance building in a renaissance garden.

These renaissance gardens, carefully planned by geometry, seem to most English visitors artificial and perhaps mechanical. Sometimes, perhaps, they seemed so to the French and the English style of garden, with its winding paths and carefully contrived naturalism, became popular in France also. You may find both kinds of garden together, the two making a delightful contrast.

In the periods in which the châteaux were neglected the gardens quickly fell into ruin. A few seasons of neglect would destroy the geometrical renaissance garden.

Today many of the châteaux have gardens beautiful in season, but not pretending to preserve the renaissance idea. In a few instances the renaissance garden has been reconstructed. The most notable are at Chenonceau and Villandry (plate 29). At Chenonceau the gardens of Diane de Poitier and of Catherine de Médicis blossom as perhaps those ladies saw them. At Villandry a very large and intricate parterre garden has been reconstructed.

The topographical approach to the châteaux is satisfactory for the traveller, but less so for those interested in the history of architecture who wish to study the development of function and style. In the following lists the châteaux we visit in this book are grouped broadly according to architectural style.

Medieval châteaux, that is to say fortified castles
Angers
Beaugency: Caesar's tower
Chinon
Cinq-mars
Lavardin
Loches
Luynes
Montbazon
Montoire
Plessis-Bourré
Plessis-Macé
Sully-sur-Loire
Trèves

Transitional châteaux, i.e. gothic with renaissance detail
Baugé
Beaugency
Blois—wings of Charles d'Orléans and Louis XII
Fougères-sur-Bièvre
Gien
Langeais
Loches: later part
Montsoreau

Plessis-lès-Tours
Saumur
Talcy
Ussé

Renaissance châteaux, retaining gothic plan or detail
Amboise
Azay-le-Rideau
Blois: François 1 wing
Brissac
Chambord
Chenonceau
Durtal
Le Lude
La Possonière
Serrant
Villandry
Villesavin

Classical châteaux
Beauregard
Blois: Gaston d'Orléans wing
Cheverny
Ménars
Montgeoffroy
Poncé

PART ONE

The Orléanais and the Blésois
Gien to Chaumont

The Orléanais

The Orléanais, the *pagus Aurelianensis* of the Romans, takes its name from the city of Orléans, which in turn is named after one or other of the Roman emperors Marcus Aurelius or Aurelian. As a province its boundaries may not have been distinct, and they remain vague today, when the ancient province is split between the *départements* of Eure-et-Loir, Loiret, and Loir-et-Cher. We are not concerned with those boundaries in this book, except on the western side, where it is convenient to accept the modern departmental boundary between Loir-et-Cher and Indre-et-Loire as the boundary between the Orléanais and Touraine. This includes within the Orléanais the district around Blois, which is known as the Blésois.

The Orléanais contains the great arc of the Loire, with Orléans at its most northerly point, that converts the river from the northerly course it has so far followed to a direction generally west. The district within the arc, called Sologne, is heavily wooded and thick with lakes, a favourite hunting ground for sportsmen of many kinds—boar and deer hunters, wild-fowlers, fishermen. It is cut through by the main motor-road, the N20, between Orléans and Vierzon, and patterned by a maze of minor roads, which yet seem to leave the solitudes of the Sologne solitary still. This is country that is often described as mournful, and in the autumn it may well deserve the epithet.

Sologne contrasts with the smiling valley of the Loire. The river brings light and warmth, as though the sun of the south flowed down with the water from the mountains of the Massif

Central to flood the lower land with a light reflected between water and sky.

Towns, villages, monasteries, and châteaux rose and flourished along the course of the river, or declined as times and fashion changed. Gien is the first of our châteaux, but it is now much reduced in size. Châteauneuf, too, is residual. Orléans is gone. Whatever château there was at Orléans, in which the counts of Paris and the dukes of Orléans may have lived when they visited their fiefs, is not now in evidence—there is only the sixteenth-century Hôtel de Ville, no more than a house, in which now and then a monarch or a prince stayed for a while. For us the châteaux may be said to begin again with Beaugency, but that was never large. It is around Blois, in the Blésois, that the concentration is encountered, with Blois itself, Chambord, Cheverny, Chaumont, and Ménars, and with Amboise and Chenonceau just beyond the border in Touraine.

North of the river lies the Gâtinais, much of which is wooded, and the Beauce country, with its wheatfields stretching up to Chartres and beyond. Part of this is watered by the Loir, which comes down through Châteaudun and Vendôme to flow by way of Montoire, Troo, and Poncé on its way into Anjou and to Angers. This, too, has not a great deal to offer to the seeker after châteaux. Montoire and Poncé have châteaux and La Possonière a manor house, the home of the Ronsard family. We visit them, not in this section, but on our return journey.

2. Gien to Orléans

The nearness of Paris to the Loire valley is as convenient for modern tourists as it was for the kings of France. Package tours from England in many instances pause in Paris for a day or two before going on to the Loire. That is excellent if time is sufficient, but to divide a short holiday between Paris and the Loire valley is not just to either place. The Loire valley is large and complex and needs at least a fortnight to see only the better-known châteaux and churches in reasonable comfort. On this assumption we shall start from Paris in order to reach conveniently the little town of Gien, the beginning of our exploration. Refresh yourself there with the wines of Sancerre or of Pouilly-Fumé, for the sufficient reason that they come from grapes grown on the slopes a few miles higher up the river; and because their cool sharpness, slightly sweet, is an introduction to the many excellent wines of the Loire.

The little town climbs a steep hill above the sandy Loire, which is crossed by a handsome bridge of several arches—it is worth walking across the bridge to see, from the farther shore, the château, the church, and the river combining into an attractive ensemble.

Louis XI gave Gien to his daughter Anne de Beaujeu, who on her father's death became regent of France during the minority of her brother Charles VIII. She built the château of Gien in 1484 on the site of one of Charlemagne's castles. It is of brick, boldly patterned in brick of a different colour, under sharply ridged slate roofs of gothic steepness, in which are tall dormers. Round turrets and the steep roofs confer an air of the middle ages on what is essentially a renaissance château. The patterning in brick is our first perception of a style that led to some remarkable developments in the desire to avoid a plain wall.

The château passed through several hands and suffered alterations, and it was badly damaged during the Hitler war. What remains today, two wings on an L plan, is only part of the original château. For a long time a prison, it became in 1952 a hunting museum. People who like killing animals for pleasure will find a lot to interest them in the château of Gien. With time to spare they may pass on to the not very distant moated château of La Bussière, which is now a museum of fishing.

The church of Saint-Jeanne d'Arc rises next to the château, within the angle of the L. Its fifteenth-century tower, capped by a steep pyramid roof, is of the date of the château, but the church attached to it is modern, a rebuilding after a bomb had destroyed the old church. It is a splendid success, in red brick, with an imposing interior whose weight neither stifles nor oppresses.

At Gien we are in what is regarded as the first of the true towns of our Loire valley. The soft air, the light of the sun, the colour of the river have a quality that belongs to the valley of the châteaux. Is it imagination, poetic fancy? I wonder. The river in this valley, gentler than in the higher reaches, and flowing more lazily, reflects the skies. The clear sunlight has something of the sharp edges of the farther south, perceptible in the cool shadows under the tall horse-chestnut trees.

We cross the river by the bridge at Gien and take the road for Sully, where the château is in strong contrast. It is a four-teenth-century castle beside the Loire, in a moat that derives its water from the river. Set beside the town suspension bridge, its white walls, its machicolations, its *poivrière* roofs, its covered *chemin de ronde* or wall-walk proclaim it a castle of an advanced design. Yet its history is slight. Joan of Arc was here briefly in 1429 and in 1430. In 1602 the castle, with a large estate, was bought by Maximilien de Béthune, who was created Duc de Sully. Favourite of Henri iv and an extremely hard-working minister, he retired to Sully and wrote his memoirs here. His study, decorated in renaissance style, may be seen.

In France, camping is considered an important pastime and sites are not hidden away in obscure fields. There is a site here beside the river, among young trees in the shelter of the château.

We cross the bridge to take the D60 and the eight kilometres to Saint-Benoît. The countryside is an airy agricultural plain with skies that descend, it seems, to shoulder height to meet the low horizon. Here and there a farm or a house, or a grove of trees, strives to break the monotony of the view. Suddenly the eye is riveted by a distant group of a different character, roof surmounting roof to a square pyramid, from which rises a graceful spire. It is the abbey church of Saint-Benoît.

It was once the abbey of Fleury. Founded in the seventh century, it grew famous for its scribes, its scholars, and its learning in matters both sacred and profane. It became the abbey of Saint-Benoît about the year 672, when the abbot, hearing that the abbey of Montecassino in Italy had been wrecked by the barbarians, sent an expedition of monks to recover the bones of Saint Benedict and of Benedict's sister Saint Scholastica, who had died there a hundred and thirty years ealier, and to bring them to Fleury. The bones are at Saint-Benoît to this day.

What was once an extensive abbey has shrunk to a tiny village centring on the ancient abbey church. At the end of a short side street or *place*, bordered by pollard limes, you come to this marvellous church, making its tremendous statements of antiquity, devotion, and architectural splendour with the modesty of a quiet aside. It is not the church of Fleury. Rebuilt during the tenth and eleventh centuries, the style is simple romanesque and the detail engaging. It is full of remarkable carving, on capitals, on walls. Before the church, and attached to it, is a broad square tower, the lower stage of which is the porch. The tower stands on pillars the capitals of which are carved with a simple devotion and a simple skill that expresses the innocence and the vision of a child. Enter the church and before looking at the nave go directly to the south transept, where there is a shrine or casket, a steamer-trunk-like box carved on the exterior with the same naïveté as the capitals in the porch. But now look up to the capitals of the choir. Here is the same devotion, the same candid vision, but with the subtlety of a more competent sculptor who could give to stone the soft folds of drapery. It is twelfth-century work, of about the same period as the porch, but this is the sanctuary and here the abbot employed his best man.

Beneath the sanctuary is a crypt, with radiating chapels and plain-ribbed vaults that lead the eye to a central pillar. In that pillar, the focus of attention, are apertures through which you may see the casket containing the bones of Saint Benedict and his sister.

Above the ground again, notice the differences between the choir and the nave. In the choir and the sanctuary round-headed arches rise to round arcades and a round-arched roof. In the nave the arches are pointed. The nave dates from the twelfth century and the pointed arch had arrived. Not steeply pointed yet, but it was on the way to a whole new style of architecture.

A few kilometres north of Saint-Benoît we can see something of the past quite as remarkable. Here, at the back of the dusty yellow *place* of Germigny-des-Prés, rises a curious little church with an antique hoariness and roughness of masonry. The first impression of great age is not altogether trustworthy, for the building was heavily restored in the nineteenth century. The church comprises a nave, a central tower over apsed transepts, and an apsed sanctuary. The nave is a later addition; originally the church was probably quatrefoil, with apses in all four directions, after the manner of a Byzantine church. It was built about the year AD 800 by Theodulf, a Catalan who was Bishop of Orléans and a minister of Charlemagne, as the chapel of a large and luxurious episcopal mansion. This house was said

5. The château of Beaugency

6. The ninth-century church of Germigny-des-Prés

7. A sculptor restoring romanesque detail at Orléans. Unrestored areas may be seen above the new panels. A few surviving sound panels provided the pattern for the new work

to be the most lavish in Neustria. The mansion has disappeared and nothing in the village now suggests the magnificence of that distant time except one thing, and that is in the church. Come inside. The brown stone of the four close-set vertical pillars beneath the tower surrounds us, succinctly expressing the limitations of the round romanesque arch, but the weight and the severity are softened by the curves of the apses and the half-domes they contain. In the eastern apse, filling the half-dome, is that last surviving piece from the far splendour of Germigny. It is a colourful mosaic, of the date of the church, in which two large winged angels, their heads haloed in gold rimmed with black, hover over the Arc of the Covenant. Beneath their feet is an inscription recording the foundation of the church by Theodulf.

Do not let the beauty of the mosaic lead you to neglect another piece of this church, a fifteenth-century group carved in wood, showing Saint Anne teaching the boy Jesus to read in a book open on her lap. The sculptor found his models in the neighbourhood and shows them in the costume of his time. It is a homely piece, and excellent.

Four and a half kilometres bring us to Châteauneuf-sur-Loire, a fresh, stone-built little town that suffered much during the war and was rebuilt as it was before. It has a variety of hotels and shops and makes a good centre from which to explore this upper part of the Loire valley from Gien to Orléans. The 'new' château that gave the town its name was built in the seventeenth century, in place of an earlier one, by La Vrillière, whose marble mausoleum is in the church. La Vrillière would be saddened to see what has happened to his château since. A man called Lebrun bought it for a song after the Revolution and demolished most of it. A tower under a dome, the kitchens, stables, and an orangery remain to show that La Vrillière's château was of considerable size. The Musée de la Marine de la Loire now occupies the ground floor, and here you may see something of the methods by which rivermen ascended and descended the shallow river.

The church in the town dates from the twelfth century. Its ancient tower stands still, attached to an open-sided arcaded space that was the nave; the present nave comes next to this space. La Vrillière's monument is, as it was intended to be, the most imposing thing in this church.

A busy main road, the N152, runs from Châteauneuf into Orléans. A less-congested approach may be made by crossing the Loire on the slender suspension bridge at Châteauneuf on to the D11 to Tigy and then on the D14 and D13 to Sandillon, from which the N751 comes into Orléans along the southern quay, the Quai des Augustins. The medieval bridge crossed the river from this quay. The bridge was defended on the south side by the fort of the Tourelles, near which stood the monastery of the Augustins, which the English had fortified. Joan of Arc arrived here and was astonished, so the chroniclers tell us, to find that the city of Orléans was on the other side of the river.

The city was then held by the English under the command of the Earl of Salisbury. The earl was killed by, so legend says, a mischievous French boy, who applied fire to the touch-hole of a cannon just to see what would happen—the ball removed Salisbury's head. The defeat of the English was partly due to a superstitious fear by the English soldiers of the French sorceress from Domrémy. They thought they had won when one of them put an arrow through Joan's shoulder, but, wrenching it out, she came on, and that was enough to convince the English of her supernatural powers.

The capture of Orléans by Joan has been celebrated on the 7th and 8th of May ever since. The city goes into a frenzy made up partly of devotion to the memory of Joan, partly of processions and general jollities, and partly of firework displays. The several statues of Joan, none of them ancient, are decked with flowers and tricolours for the occasion.

The most prominent feature in the view across the Loire from the Quai des Augustins is the cathedral, with an airy central flèche and a pair of extraordinary west towers more remarkable than beautiful; they seem to be in a quandary trying to decide for themselves whether they are gothic or renaissance. The two upper stages are open to the air and consist each of a kind of crown surrounded by slender pillars. It is not, however, the cathedral Joan saw. That cathedral, founded in the thirteenth century, suffered severely in the wars of religion. In the sixteenth century a reconstruction was begun, which was to be very long drawn out—the cathedral was still rebuilding in the nineteenth century. The gothic style was followed throughout, except for the tops of the towers, and the building has a fine air of antiquity. Its true antiquity is indicated in the crypt, where a few stones remain from the three previous cathedrals on the site, going back to the time of Charlemagne.

In order to reach the cathedral we cross the George v bridge, a victim of the French passion for renaming things: the bridge dates, not from the England of 1910, but from 1760. It was built a few yards downstream from the medieval bridge it replaced. For some reason the inhabitants were suspicious of its safety. Madame de Pompadour, whose château at Ménars was not far distant, decided to demonstrate that the bridge was safe and she crossed it in her carriage. A wit promptly declaimed:

> *Critics of our bridge, you whose impertinence*
> *Borders on temerity,*
> *The poet by a single fact reduces you to silence:*
> *This bridge is solid, for today it has carried*
> *The heaviest burden in France.*

This was a reference to the vast sums given by kings to their favourites, money provided out of taxation. The French Revolution was a long time in gestation.

The bridge leads into the Rue Royale. Off this to the right runs the Rue de la Bourgogne, in a side street off which is the reputed house of Diane de Poitiers. This is an attribution more romantic than accurate; the house is in fact a sixteenth-century renaissance hôtel, the Hôtel Cabu; it is now the home of the history museum.

Return along the street and cross the Rue Royale into the

Rue du Tabour and the Place de Gaulle, passing the sixteenth-century house that now contains the Charles Péguy Museum. In the *place* stands a picturesque building with a front elaborately timbered—a reconstruction of the house in which Joan of Arc is reputed to have stayed; the original was destroyed in 1940. The brief Rue Hallebarde now brings us into the Place du Martroi, where a mid nineteenth-century statue of Joan reigns over a swirling maze of traffic. We are in the heart of the commercial and shopping centre of Orléans.

The Rue d'Escures, on the far side of the square, leads to the Place de l'Étape, where the Hôtel de Ville is prefaced by another statue of Joan, standing with head bowed in prayer; it was sculpted by Princesse Marie d'Orléans, daughter of King Louis-Philippe. The Hôtel de Ville is a renaissance house of 1550, considerably restored—one of many buildings of the period to be found in the streets of Orléans. It was a home of French kings and queens from François II to Henri IV. It is worth penetrating behind it to find a pretty little garden, full of flowers, against the wall of which stands the gothic façade of the old chapel of Saint-Jacques.

It is worth while too to walk around the outside of the cathedral, the building of which is successively older the farther you go east. The east end itself presents that ensemble of apses, roofs, flying buttresses, and windows that the French call a *chevet*, a word for which, surprisingly, since we have the thing itself, there is no equivalent in English. You may get a good view of the cathedral *chevet* from the garden of the public library. At the bottom of the garden are some slight remnants of the Gallo-Roman town wall. The library building was the bishop's house, built in the seventeenth century, and you may go in to see an interesting staircase and carved woodwork.

The narrow Rue de la Bourgogne, by which Joan of Arc entered Orléans in triumph in 1429, will bring you, along its exiguous pavements, back to the Rue Royale.

Orléans is a city for rosarians, that is rose-lovers. Its town gardens are colourful and scented with roses. A mile or two south of the Loire and of its tributary the Loiret, at Orléans-la-Source, where a whole new suburb and a university have appeared, there is an extensive floral park, where roses from all over the world may be seen. The 'source' is the river Loiret, which, diving underground some miles distant, comes up to the light again here.

3. Orléans to Fougères

We leave Orléans along the south side of the river, past the camping-site and the racecourse, to take the N751 south-west. We are in a countryside beloved of Louis xi, who chose to be interred and to have his monument in the church of Notre-Dame at Cléry-Saint-André. Cléry, as was Orléans too, was on the route of the pilgrims trudging through France towards Spain and the shrine of Saint James of Compostela. On such routes a lot of money flowed by in the scrips and packs of pilgrims, some of which might be diverted to Cléry if only there were a shrine or holy image at which those pilgrims might feel dutifully bound to stop and worship. But, it seems, a holy image had to come by miracle, or at least by good fortune. The pattern is repeated in dozens of places. A statue miraculously arrives or is fortuitously found near by. At Cléry a figure of the Virgin and Child was discovered in a bush by ploughmen, in 1280. Its fame grew quickly and pilgrims paused to venerate the figure and to make their contribution, by which one step on their road to salvation might be assured. The little church then at Cléry proved too small for the growing number of pilgrims and a larger church was built. This second church was destroyed in 1428 by the Earl of Salisbury.

Charles vii and the bastard Dunois (the friend and companion in arms of Joan of Arc) contributed money to build a new church. Later, Louis xi and Charles viii continued the work.

The church of Notre-Dame is built in a clear and noble gothic style. As was the general custom, the building was begun at the east end. By the time the west end was under construction the Renaissance had arrived and the two flanking doorways have low basket arches, from which gothic pinnacles rise to a triangular gothic traceried window. In the hollow chamfers of the doorways companies of martins find fortunate sites for their adhesive nests, and as you look at man's architecture and theirs dark, curious little heads pop out from their cups of mud and regard you warily as though defying comparison of their work.

Inside the church the holy image of the Virgin and Child, on the modern altar, is covered by a mantle through which only the heads appear. In the nave, under one of the arcades, the monument of Louis XI is set at an angle so that the kneeling figure of the king shall exactly face the statue. The bones of the king and those of his wife Charlotte de Savoie lie in a crypt below the floor, or rather their skulls do. Or what *may* be their skulls, for there are said to have been four or five of them a century ago. Also buried here is the body of that Tanguy du Châtel who wrapped up the young Dauphin and fled with him before the advancing Burgundians. The heart of that Dauphin's son Charles VIII is here too.

In the choir a series of misericordes show a number of different grotesque faces, not gothic but renaissance. They were given by Henri II, who had his initials and those of his mistress Diane de Poitiers carved on some of them.

Dunois, according to Bernard Shaw, Joan's 'Jack Dunois', has a chapel on the south side of the church. Perhaps more immediately interesting is the chapel of Saint-Jacques, a very fine and rich renaissance structure the decoration of which includes representations of pilgrims' staffs and scrips and of the cords they tied around their waists to gather in their loose-fitting pilgrim gowns.

Louis XI had a house to the south of the church. It is still there and is now a school.

Leave Cléry by the minor road towards the Loire. It crosses the river to Meung-sur-Loire, a town known for two poets. One of them, Jean de Meung, is commemorated by a modern statue of quite extraordinary lack of inspiration. Jean, writing at the beginning of the fourteenth century, extended the then century-old *Roman de la Rose* by a further eighteen thousand verses— the original poem was four thousand verses long. The other poet was François Villon, whose history is studded with the names of prisons. He was imprisoned in Meung in the now-ruined tower next to the eleventh-century church, under sentence of death for some misdemeanour, until in October 1461 Louis XI entered the town and proclaimed an amnesty for prisoners. Only the previous year Villon had been in prison in Orléans, also under sentence of death, to be equally fortunate on the passage of the little princess of Orléans through the town in July. Villon's poems suggest regret for a life mis-spent, but misfortune and trouble seem to have pursued him constantly.

Villon would have known Beaugency, for in his day this small town possessed the only bridge over the Loire between Orléans and Blois. Built on a hillside above the river, Beaugency's streets and squares slope so that the visitor constantly feels that he has one leg shorter than the other. The slopes drop down to the old town, which in a compact space manages to retain an atmosphere of antiquity that seems only to have thickened with time. Nowhere can one so easily think oneself back into the sixteenth century and even farther, into the middle ages. Towering over everything is a gigantic square *donjon*, with the verticals of flat buttresses against the walls and few and irregular openings between them. This is the Tour de César, built in the eleventh century and a shell since the interior was burnt out by the Protestants in 1567. At its foot is a small *place*, sloping down to a gate in the town wall. To the left of this gate is the comfortable little château of Dunois, the bastard of Orléans. Dunois was the son of Louis Duke of Orléans, who brought the infant Jean home with him one day to be reared by his wife with the rest of his family at Blois. Little Jean may have been a heartache to the wife who adopted him as one of her own children; she could not know how Dunois would become a

8. An approach to the cathedral of Saint-Louis at Blois

9. Fougères-sur-Bièvre – small château or manor-house?

10. Chambord: renaissance magnificence

11. The classical symmetry of Cheverny

12. The stables at Chaumont – the conical building in the corner was originally a pigeon-house

mighty soldier faithful to his half-brother Charles through many tribulations and through the long exile of Charles in England—and faithful to Joan of Arc. Without Dunois Joan could not have gained the success and renown she did. The château is now a museum of the art and traditions of the Orléanais.

Opposite the château rises the twelfth-century church of Notre-Dame, once the church of an abbey. It lost its stone roof at the time of the fire that burned out the interior of the Tour de César, and another rather curious roof was built of wood.

Wander about the small and errant streets of Beaugency as you will—there are other things to be discovered, such as the detached tower without a church, or the charming renaissance Hôtel de Ville.

The château of Talcy is set inland, away from the river, among minor country roads. It is a minor château, but it is a pleasant one. This is the house that Bernard Salviati wanted so desperately to fortify—and yet never did, perhaps because the prestige of fortification was specifically disallowed in the licence granted by the king. Nevertheless, the *donjon* of the château *is* fortified, with machicolations and a covered *chemin-de-rond*. The *donjon* looks out, on the south side, over the upland plain of the Beauce and on the inside into a small courtyard containing an attractive covered well of renaissance design. The house is furnished with period furnishings.

Talcy, the plain little château of Talcy, has poetic associations. Bernard Salviati's daughter, briefly encountered by Ronsard, was celebrated by him under the name of Cassandre; Salviati's grand-daughter Diane provided the same inspiration for Agrippa d'Aubigné. Diane married, however, one Guillaume de Musset, and thereby became the ancestress of Alfred de Musset.

Ronsard had an acute eye for beauty and a sense of the sadness of time passing. It was perhaps for Cassandre (but more probably for Hélène de Surgères) that he wrote:

> *Quand vous serez bien vieille, au soir, à la chandelle,*
> *Assise auprès du feu, devidant et filant,*
> *Direz, chantant mes vers, en vous emerveillant:*
> *Ronsard me célébroit du temps que j'estois belle.*

a poem the echoes of which are found in Yeats's:

> *When you are old and grey and full of sleep*
> *And nodding by the fire, take down this book,*
> *And slowly read, and dream of the soft look*
> *Your eyes had once, and of their shadows deep.*

The gothicism of Talcy as Salviati restored it was already out of date in his time. He had bought the house in 1517. It was only two years before the beginning of Chambord, François I's renaissance extravaganza in the soggy forests south of the Loire. Today those forests are, for miles, conifer plantations, but in François's time the dominant tree was the oak. Under the green and angular boughs quantities of wild game browsed in the dappled sunlight, peaceful and withdrawn. Occasionally disturbed by the stealthy tracker seeking out a fine specimen for the benefit of the hunt, they would explode into flight as the horns of the hunters sounded among the trees. Ferocious wild boar haunted the recesses and sometimes turned upon their hunters. There were wolves too—the name of Blois comes from a Celtic word meaning 'wolf'. Wolves were still to be found in the eighteenth century—John Evelyn had hoped to see one—but they are gone now. There are still boars in the woods, however, if the warning signs by the roadside are to be believed.

The château of Chambord is not the most beautiful of the Loire châteaux, either in its architecture or in its site, but who does not remember Chambord as the most outstanding experience of the Loire valley. And despite the fact that it is for the most part a great empty barracks, with only a few of its four hundred rooms furnished. One of its attractions for me is that once having paid the entrance fee, you may wander freely about this extraordinary château, through the echoing chambers and up the enchanting double spiral stairway to the complex roof, without the restraint and the boredom of a guide. In most of the châteaux of the Loire valley you are compelled to join a party under the tutelage of a guide. He carries a large bunch of keys to lock the door by which you enter a room and to unlock that by which you go out, so that you are imprisoned with him in each room. This officious procedure does not happen at Chambord.

Yet this freedom is only a minor part of the interest of Chambord. At the back of every visitor's perception of the château is a nagging question—what on earth was it for? Within a few years of the commencement of building François I had decided to transfer the court to Paris. The builders were still struggling with the foundations in the swampy ground, pushing in enormous quantities of hardcore and hammering in hundreds of piles. The work could have been stopped. But it went on throughout the reign of François I and into that of Henri II, even though it was then obvious that the place would never be occupied for more than a few days at a time in the spring and summer. In winter the damp and the chill were unbearable. Chambord was, in fact, in modern terms nothing more than a holiday villa, or in the terms of the period a hunting-box.

In plan it is an unoriginal medieval castle, exceptional only in the scale of its elements. Basically it is a keep with corner towers, set in a walled bailey. The originality is in the decoration and in the design of the double spiral staircase.

The wooded Parc de Chambord is co-extensive with the Forêt de Boulogne, which perhaps got its name from the wood to the west of Paris. You approach from the north through a canyon of trees and suddenly a section of the façade of the château appears, with its exciting grouping of chimneys and pinnacles over the central *donjon*. As you come more into the open in front of the château, the huge size impresses, seen across the restricted stream of the diverted Cosson (plate 10). When the château was built it stood in a moat that lapped the walls, and the splendid façade and its roof were doubled in the water; but the moat has been filled in. The façade is symmetrical, with the central *donjon* connected on each side by a gallery over arcades to a fat corner tower. The tower on the left, however, has a projection where the gallery joins, a minor detail but a detraction from the symmetry; it was part of the quarters of François I. Perhaps he had it built so in order that, while living in the château, he could still see the splendour of the *donjon*.

That imposing frontage has only a small door. You have to—and kings had to—go round the back to enter by the Porte Royale into the courtyard.

The plan of the *donjon* needs a word of introduction. Straight up the centre rises the famous staircase in the two flights of its double spiral. You may amuse yourself with your companions by starting on different spirals, as Mlle de Montpensier, the Grande Mademoiselle, did with her father, running up and down with him in a game of hide and seek. On each floor are four large chambers arranged spokewise from the staircase in the form of a cross. They are called guard-rooms for want of a better term. They are impressive but not particularly useful. Notice in each of these rooms or guard-chambers the interesting panelled ceilings with the salamander of François I prominent in the decoration. Between the arms of the cross and the corner towers are the apartments.

One suite of rooms is furnished and hung with tapestries and pictures appropriate to the château. It is well worth attention in order to have an idea how this great and echoing, cold, stone château might have been softened and made habitable by its furnishings. A massive porcelain stove shows how heating was attempted.

You may climb up the staircase to walk on narrow paths among the domes, the chimneys, the cupolas, and the ornament of the celebrated roof. It is a curious experience. There is something of theatre, of the fairground about it, with everything rather coarser than you supposed—the detail is, in fact, adapted to the scale of the building. Some of the ornament consists of slate panels let into the white stone for contrast.

The various inhabitants of Chambord occupied the house at long intervals. François I, of course, used it, and in 1539 he received the Emperor Charles v here, and greatly enjoyed the wonder and the amazement of his guest. François filled the place with women, elaborately gowned, and took the trouble to scratch on a window his discovery that 'Toute femme varie, bien folle qui s'y fie'—'All women are fickle; he is a fool who trusts them.' Other kings came in turn. Louis XIII gave Chambord (and Blois) in 1626 in appanage to his untrustworthy brother Gaston d'Orléans, father of the engaging Grande Mademoiselle. Louis XIV put mansard roofs on the low buildings of the courtyard; these roofs have since been removed. A century later the exiled King of Poland, Stanislas Leczinski, was given Chambord for a dwelling and he lived here for seven years. He was succeeded in 1748 by the Maréchal de Saxe, reputed victor of that curious battle of Fontenoy; the *maréchal* kept a company of soldiers here and liked to review them regularly, punishing severely any man who did not satisfy him. Napoleon gave the château to another marshal, Berthier, who sold the furniture and allowed parts of the building to fall into ruin.

The château was then put on sale. It was bought by public subscription and presented to the infant Duc de Bordeaux, grandson of Charles x and heir to the throne—some of his toys may be seen in the appartments; he took the title of Comte de Chambord. After the troubles of 1870 there was a move to offer the count the throne, but he insisted that the white flag of the Bourbons should replace the tricolour. The French would not have that and France became, as it has since remained, a republic. The Comte de Chambord died in exile.

Seven kilometres south of Chambord, on the edge of the Forêt de Boulogne, a superintendent of works for Chambord, Jean le Breton, built himself a château in every way a contrast with Chambord. It was 1537 and Chambord was not yet complete. Villesavin is a small château, little more than a *gentilhommière*, modest in size and modest in demeanour, but in style years ahead of its big neighbour. The symbols of defence were ignored at Villesavin. The round corner towers give way to square and domestic pavilions, the deterrent aspect to one of pleasant invitation. The main block is of five bays only, and technically of only one storey, though there is another ample storey above in the large and steeply sloped roof. The dormer windows in this roof have ornate pediments above them, a detail we shall encounter again in our consideration of renaissance châteaux. Villesavin is furnished with many exhibits of interest. It has, too, a pigeon-house, in which the revolving *potence* or ladder by which the nests were reached is still intact.

We pursue the developing renaissance style another seven or eight kilometres westwards, to the triangle between the junction of the N765 and the N156, where the château of Beauregard is found. This little château, built between 1545 and 1553 by Jean De Thier, a secretary of state to Henri II, takes the classical idiom, perceptible at Villesavin, a step further. The steep roofs of the gothic legacy remain, but the dormers are simpler and square-headed windows proclaim a different future, a more restrained elegance, confirmed in the use of Doric and Ionic columns and a careful sense of proportion. The house is notable for a gallery of 363 historical portraits and a tile floor illustrating an army of the seventeenth century.

The logical end to the development of the château that we are pursuing is the full-blown classical style, and we find it only a few kilometres to the south-east, at Cheverny. Many of the châteaux of the Loire valley, even Chambord, grew into existence through changes of style and of fashion, through neglect and restoration, through demolition and extension, and the result is evident in a perception of humanity, in a state of poised excitement, of expectation. Cheverny is just the opposite of all this. It was carefully designed, completed in a single build—*d'un seul jet*—in 1634, and it has been occupied by the same family ever since (the present owner is the Marquis de

Vibraye). All this shows. The château is aristocratic, peaceful, and still, even self-complacent in its perfection of plan and of façade, in its clear white stone under blue-grey roofs and domes of slate. Even the furnishing inside dates largely from the seventeenth century, as though time and change had no power here.

The house is open, but only partly. You are conducted rapidly through five or six magnificent rooms, thickly furnished with all sorts of beautiful and valuable things; very probably you will be part of a group filling the rooms so crowdedly that you have difficulty in moving around, and if so you will emerge, as we did, thoroughly unsatisfied and probably disgruntled. Outside you will find that notices in the park confine your steps to the entrance path and the broad central drive. There is an old pigeon-house, but you are not allowed into it. You *are* allowed into a 'museum of the hunt', which turns out to be a hall the walls of which are covered with antlers, memorials of the gory successes of generations of the family.

The high price of entrance to Cheverny and the little that one gets for it deals a blow to one's enjoyment of the châteaux of the Loire valley. We can re-establish that enjoyment by going a little aside of the general way, to Fougères-sur-Bièvre, about twelve kilometres to the south-west of Cheverny. The little château here stands in the village, and close by its walls the modest Bièvre ripples clear and clean, inhabited by trout, which you may watch from the bridge. The château, built from 1470, takes little notice of the newfangled niceties of the Renaissance, then just becoming known in France. It is dourly gothic. Only a dormer window with a fanciful top and a few windows with transoms and mullions betray the new fashion, and these come from changes in the sixteenth century. The rest is of the middle ages, frowning possessively and paternally over the town from the *poivrière* roofs of round turrets and towers, from covered wall-walks, and from heavy machicolation.

The château was built by Pierre de Refuge, treasurer to Louis XI, as a country house and also, as you may still clearly see, as a farmhouse, the centre of an estate. Long neglected, and in the nineteenth century a wire-works, the château has been sensibly restored, but it contains little furniture. You must be accompanied by a guide, but here we found the guide a knowledgeable man, a villager whose interest in the building had survived a thousand repetitions of its story. He took us round the whole château, climbing the towers into the midst of the astounding carpentry of the *poivrière* roofs, along the narrow passages (the *chemin de ronde*) above the machicolations, whose apertures gave a limited view straight down the sheer walls, and into the living chambers and the great hall. The château, if not a convenient house, could be lived in again, and I wish it were. Something of the spirit and of the personality of its builder hangs around it still, but it needs the warmth of present habitation.

4. Blois to Chaumont

In Fougères I asked a native of the town for directions for the road to Blois and had my pronunciation corrected. 'Bool-wah' said my informant, giving the sound between b and l considerable value and a tonic accent. I remarked this pronunciation elsewhere, and in the town of Blois itself.

Blois is a large and busy town with inclined streets that descend to the Place Victor Hugo below the high, arcaded façade, set on a rocky cliff, of the François I wing of the château. The buildings about here are for the most part modern-commercial, but among them, near the square, are the fifteenth-century pavilion of Anne de Bretagne and the fifteenth-century brick and stone Hôtel d'Alluye, built for Florimund Robertet, who was also the builder of the important but ill-fated château of Bury outside the town.

A number of interesting houses exist in the old quarter near the cathedral, nodding over narrow streets that are sometimes so steep as to need stairs. You climb them head down and panting, and suddenly look up to find your view closed by a massive wall of stone in which are set openings of pointed gothic and of round-arched renaissance character, one above the other (plate 8). This is the cathedral. The conjunction of styles derives from the destruction of the nave and the choir by a storm in the seventeenth century. The consequent rebuilding was carried out in the mode of the time. There was no tendency here towards the conscious archaism that is to be seen at Orléans. There the cathedral, still building in the seventeenth century, at the same time as the cathedral of Blois, kept new work in gothic to marry with what already existed. At Blois the lower parts of the building that survived the storm are thirteenth and fourteenth century, with the pointed arches and the flamboyant ornament of their day. The rebuilt upper parts, by contrast, have the round arches of the Renaissance. The origins of the cathedral are older than either of these: the crypt is romanesque, of the tenth century.

It is rewarding to continue round the cathedral, along the north side, to a long terrace to the east, filled with flower-beds. The view from the terrace is wide, with a reach of the river extending from a graceful modern bridge upstream down to the early seventeenth-century town bridge designed by the elder Gabriel. Gabriel's bridge took the place of a house-encumbered medieval bridge that was swept away by the Loire in one of those winter floods that seem so unlikely in the shallow summer aspect of the river. It was the possession of a bridge in a time when bridges over the Loire were few and far between that made Blois a place of importance commercially and militarily. The suburb south of the river, however, never grew large. Now its blue-grey slate roofs shine against a background of dark green, the woods of the Forêt de Russy only a little distance away, clothing a long, low hillside.

Downstream of the bridge the château rises on a rocky mount, a superb site. The Place du Château, reached by steep, winding streets, and once the forecourt of the château, is now a car park for visitors, with pollard trees to give shade. It overlooks from a high terrace an airy view of the Loire and of Gabriel's bridge, through which the water flows with a gentle rush to swirl around young trees growing on the drifts formed in the eddies below the piers.

Across the west end of the *place* is the entrance wing of the château, the wing built by Louis xii. You ought to stand and look at this façade. Blois was originally a medieval château; in the thirteenth century, if we may judge from what remains of that time, it was of considerable size and considerable splendour.

The finest remnant of that period is the Salle des États—the parliament hall. The tall gable beside the right-hand edge of the range belongs to this hall. The Louis XII wing, attached to the Salle des États, was built at the end of the fifteenth century, a spirited medley of gothic and renaissance detail. The walls of brick, diapered red and blue, the stone dressings round the windows, the square-headed mullioned and transomed windows themselves, and the rounded arch of the entrance flanked by ornamental pillars, derive from the Renaissance, as also, for contrast, do the ruderies of some of the carved label stops— the ornaments terminating the stone hoods of the windows. From the middle ages descend the cusped parapet along the edge of the roof, the ornate gables and pinnacles of the dormers, and the cusped, pinnacled, and crocketed double gable over the equestrian figure of Louis XII in the recess above the doorway. The horse on which the king sits raises two legs on the same side—not an impossible action, for some desert horses are taught to move in this way, as a camel does, but it is surprising to find it here. It must be deliberate, however, for a sculptor of this quality would not make so elementary an error.

The small postern door beside the larger one has above it the figure of a porcupine carrying a crown on its back, the emblem of Louis XII—there is another, smaller example over the larger door. These figures may be taken as an introduction to a number of signs and emblems scattered throughout the château and to be seen in royal châteaux elsewhere—besides the porcupine there are the cord and ermine tails of Anne de Bretagne, the ermine itself used by both Anne de Bretagne and Claude de France, and the frequently found crowned salamander of François I—a little dragon spitting fire, with a floating crown above its head, often on a background of flames. The initials L A F will be seen too, ornately drawn and each crowned. L is for Louis XII, A for his wife Anne de Bretagne, and F for François I. The crown on the F is usually sunk down on the upper bar, disguising the true shape of the letter.

We enter the château and come into a courtyard that is

the most divers and interesting among the courtyards of the
châteaux of the Loire. From the time of its purchase by Louis
d'Orléans, brother of Charles vi, in 1391, Blois may be said to
have been a royal château. It was Louis's son, the poet Charles
d'Orléans, who began the transformation of the medieval
fortress into a more comfortable house, and initiated a series
of changes that have left Blois a museum of renaissance development. All that remains of Charles's building is the two-
storeyed range to the south of the entrance wing (plate 15).
Charles introduced the arcaded gallery or cloister, divided by a
double string-course from the windows of the floor above—an
ensemble we shall find again and indeed have already seen at
Talcy.

Here, in this new building, more humane than the fortress he
had inherited, Charles, after his twenty-five years of captivity
in England, held court for poets, writers, artists, and musicians,
and, as his contemporary René of Anjou did, formed a pleasantly
civilised community. Charles, whose two previous wives had
died, married for the third time, to Marie de Clèves, a girl a
quarter of his age. Twenty years later, when Charles was
seventy-one, she gave birth to an heir. The child, named Louis,
was to become King Louis xii.

When Louis xii inherited Blois he pulled down part of his
father's building and built the east wing, the entrance wing we
see now (plate 15); but he respected in his new work the style
his father had introduced, only making it more ornate. The
arcaded gallery or cloister reappears, with pillars covered with
low-relief ornament, the double string course is there, with a
line of cusped carving, the dormers have grown gothic pinnacles. At each end of the block is a rectangular stair tower, the
larger one bearing the porcupine of Louis in a fanciful crocketed
border above the door.

But it is not the work of either Charles or Louis that immediately attracts the eye in the courtyard of Blois. The eye-catcher
is the extraordinary and deservedly famous stair tower of the wing
of François i (plate 17). François succeeded Louis xii in 1515 and

at once began to rebuild the château. His wife, Claude de France, was Louis's daughter and had spent her childhood at Blois, but whether she abetted her husband in the rebuilding or regretted the passing of things with which she was familiar it is not possible to know. Perhaps she was too occupied to think of it, for between the ages of sixteen and twenty-five she gave birth to seven children. The gay, handsome François, whose court was full of women beautifully gowned at his expense, loved his wife, and it is likely that it was her death in 1524, at the age of twenty-five, that was partly or largely responsible for his losing interest in Blois and abandoning the rebuilding.

François's wing is high renaissance, ornate, lively, and enjoyable, with none of the concessions to symmetry and historical logic that were to distinguish the later classical style. Whatever plan there may have been, it was frequently altered or amended as the building progressed. It is evident, for instance, that the famous staircase is an afterthought, tacked on to a façade already almost complete. The basic project must have come from Italy, taken over with small consideration of the different climate of the northern half of France or of the Loire valley in particular. The high, steep roofs of the French Renaissance, deriving from the gothic, are practical in a country with heavy winter rains. The staircase, on the contrary, with its open tower, is more suitable for long summers and dry seasons, and there must have been times in the weather of the Loire valley when it was unusable. Even its decoration seems to have been designed to take advantage of cast shadows from a high sun. The tower rises in four visible stages to an ornate eaves line, above which a corona stage, with a balustrade and leaning gargoyles, completes the effect.

The windows of the wing are of renaissance pattern but are spaced irregularly. They are divided by panels of irregular size, flanked by flat pilasters. The dormers above the pierced parapet are richly ornamented. Indeed, ornament is applied with a lavish hand. The salamander is everywhere, in the centre of every panel, in the pierced parapets of the staircase tower, and on the corona. Yet something in particular is evident here. Perhaps for the first time in France, the Renaissance is not merely superficial ornament of Italian origin applied to a gothic wall, as it is in earlier buildings. Despite the high slate roof, the frequent gothic detail of cusps and gargoyles, this is a renaissance building in which the architect as well as the sculptor has been aware of the influence of Italy, and through Italy, distantly, of Greece.

When François began to build, the high, thick, fortress wall of the medieval château still existed. This wall was retained. The new wing was built one room deep up against it, an economy that may appear unexpected in so free-spending a society. At some stage, certainly when the wing was well advanced, François decided to enlarge it by building to the depth of an additional room along its length on the town side. The new building was simply attached to the outer face of the medieval wall, which remains embedded in the wing like a thick spine. Doorways had to be driven through this wall, making dark and constricted passages or entries, one of which was to prove opportune for the murder of the Duc de Guise by the minions of Henri III in 1588.

The town façade of this new building, rising above the Place Victor Hugo, expresses the renaissance mode, but it has otherwise little to do with the façade on to the courtyard. It is less intimate, a little barrack-like and repetitive. Its principal feature, which has been much discussed, is two storeys of arcades, the openings of which look out from a series of individual lodges rather like theatre boxes. The design is said to have been based on one of Bramante's at the Vatican, but Bramante had galleries behind his arcades.

However, we are considering the courtyard. The fourth side, the west side, is very different from the others.

A hundred years after François I ceased to build at Blois, Louis XIII gave the château to his brother Gaston d'Orléans. Louis had no heir and it appeared that Gaston was likely to be the next king. Gaston was impatient, devious, and conspiratorial. He involved himself in several conspiracies against the king and when they were discovered exculpated himself by betraying his fellow conspirators. Louis sent him to Blois in the hope that there he would be out of the way, and in order to keep him busy supplied him with money to rebuild.

Gaston employed a notable architect, François Mansart, to design the new château he proposed to put up at Blois. The west wing, facing the château entrance across the courtyard, is the work of Gaston and Mansart (plate 16). With this wing we have passed out of the ebullience and exuberance of the early Renaissance into the reason and symmetry of classicism. The doorway is in the centre, flanked by pillars with Doric capitals, with the window above between pillars with Ionic capitals, which rise to a pediment. The windows are regularly, precisely spaced. The line of the cornice is broken centrally by a cartouche with volutes, and above is a bust. The roof retains its gothic steepness, but this has now become an element of the French classical style. Gothic ornament, gothic planning, the gothic spirit have disappeared altogether. It is architecture of a splendid kind, a beautiful example of its period, worked out in careful detail and built to a plan. As architecture it is certainly superior to anything else in the courtyard—but it just as certainly receives less attention from visitors than does the François I wing. Cameras click more frequently for François than they do for Gaston d'Orléans. This is a fact, though it may be no useful criterion of taste.

In 1638 the queen, Anne of Austria, gave birth to a son, the future Louis XIV. Gaston's chances of the throne thereby dropped to zero. He suddenly found his position of far less importance than it had been. Richelieu, Louis XIII's astute minister, stopped the money that had been flowing to Blois, and consequently the building work stopped too.

Gaston had meant to demolish the whole of the François I wing and the whole of the courtyard in order to rebuild in his new fashion. You may still see, where the new wing abuts

François's wing, the irregular masonry of the corner where the demolition ceased. The history of Blois, of grand new designs that were interrupted after they were in part realised, never to proceed further than a single wing, has left us with the story of the Renaissance in French architecture exemplified in a single courtyard, with the fifteenth-century chapel of Saint-Calais standing for the tenacious gothic mode. The chapel is the choir of a larger church, the nave of which disappeared under the pick-axes of Gaston's men.

A great deal of the interior of the château is open, but most of the rooms are empty of furniture or almost empty. You pass from room to room, from floor to floor in François's wing, admiring the noble fireplaces with his salamanders on them, and enter what was the Salle du Conseil. Into this room the Duc de Guise came early in the morning, to attend the summons of the king, Henri III. Guise had spent the night with one of the ladies of the queen's court. He had not breakfasted and was hungry, but all he could find to eat was a few Brignolais plums in a silver box. Guise was the most important man of his day, the most powerful, virtually the ruler of the country; it is possible that he meant to rule it altogether, to dethrone Henri. Guise's men were everywhere at Blois and he felt himself safe. When a friend put into his hand a paper saying that he was in danger, that someone meant him harm, he scribbled on it 'They would not dare'. But the king, a weak man driven to extremes, *did* dare. Henri still had a group of adherents, the Quarante-cinq, the Forty-five, twenty of whom he employed to assassinate Guise.

A messenger came to the duke to ask him to present himself to the king in the *cabinet vieux*, the old study. To reach this Guise had to pass through one of those narrow passages in the thick medieval wall into the king's bedroom, and from that back through the wall into the *cabinet vieux*. In the royal bedchamber Guise saw eight man, members of the Quarante-cinq, sitting about in conversation, but took no heed of them. He moved into the passage to the old study and was immedi-

13. Amboise: the panel above the chapel door showing Saint Hubert's meeting with a stag with a crucifix in its antlers

14. Chambord: the stairway

15–17. The four wings of Blois. 15 (*above*) The fifteenth-century Louis XII wing with its two towers, and to its right the earlier Charles d'Orléans wing. 17 (*right*) The stair-tower of François I's renaissance wing, early sixteenth century. 16 (*below*) Gaston d'Orléans's seventeenth-century classical wing

18. The ruins of Chinon

19. The Tour Saint-Antoine at Loches

ately attacked by twelve men with daggers. The eight men behind now in turn attacked him, imprisoning the duke's arms and winding his cloak about his sword so that he could not draw it. But Guise was a big and physically powerful man. He threw off some of the attackers and smashed the face of another with the silver box he still had in his hand. The contest was unequal. Guise staggered back into the bedchamber, bleeding from several wounds, and fell dead beside the bed. Now the king made his appearance, and looked down at the body with satisfaction. He spurned it with his foot, or, as some said, kicked the duke in the face. 'How big he is!' Henri exclaimed.

The duke's brother, the Cardinal of Lorraine, also at Blois, was arrested and held captive for the night. Next day he too was murdered. The two bodies were burned in an upper room of the château.

The *cabinet vieux* disappeared in the demolition made by Gaston d'Orléans, but the bedchamber remains, a long room with walls ornamented with arabesque patterns, and with a tall plain fireplace reaching to the painted, closely spaced beams of the ceiling.

The Louis XII wing is now a museum, which is to say that it is furnished with appropriate antique furniture, tapestries, and pictures. Here you may obtain an idea of the luxury of the court in the days of the château's habitation, of the colour and pattern that pleased the eye, of the atmosphere and movement of life in a royal palace of the Renaissance. In contrast the rooms of François's wing are cold, dim, and deserted, and the retention here of an occasional picture or tapestry, of a chair or a table does little to alleviate the bareness. Not even the arrogant ghost of the murdered Duc de Guise, rudely wrenched from its living complacency, flutters the air. But who knows, if you listen and have the right kind of extrasensory perception, you may snatch a conspiratorial whisper from the mutterings of the Quarante-cinq, you may hear the rush of feet and the shouts of the attack, the screams, the thud of a falling body, and then the ensuing wary silence, broken by the king's exclamation *'Comme il est grand!'*

Among the notable rooms that stay in the memory is the study of Catherine de Médicis. Catherine had in full measure the Italian suspicion and secretiveness of her time, and it seems to be reflected in this room. The walls are lined from floor to ceiling with beautiful panelling, carved with arabesque patterns in low relief, gilt against a background of red or blue. But many of the panels are doors to hidden cupboards, opened by pressure on a spring in the floor. We shall meet Catherine again at the château of Chaumont, and again at Chenonceau.

The last important chamber one sees in the guided tour of the château ought chronologically to be the first. It is the high and spacious hall of the Salle des États, which expresses the pure and elegant gothic of the thirteenth century. It indicates the quality of the medieval château which, in the time of Charles d'Orléans, who began the rebuilding of Blois, had seemed old and out of date.

It was probably in this noble hall that François I held the ball at which for the first time the young Pierre de Ronsard saw the teenager Cassandre Salviati and fell in love with her at once. He was an impressionable twenty years of age, she a springlike fifteen. He saw her rise, brown-haired, brown-eyed, and laughing, from a group of girls, to sing a lively song of Burgundy to the plucking of a *luth*. It was the fashion of poets of the time to celebrate ideal mistresses in their verse; Ronsard had found his ideal in the flesh. Her father married her the following year to a dull but prosperous gentleman, and she was soon a mother, but she reigned in Ronsard's verses for years afterwards.

A few kilometres upstream from Blois stands the château of Ménars. It was originally a simple country house, and a country house it still is, delightfully set in green woods, in a clearing looking out on to an unspoiled reach of the Loire, towards which its gardens descend. The river frontage is long and white and regular and classical, but not yet attaining the severity of the palladianism of the eighteenth century. The central portion, of seven bays, was built from 1637 onwards for Guillaume Charron, a man important in the service of the king. The architect Jacques-Ange Gabriel designer of the Place de la Concorde, and son of that Gabriel who designed the bridge over the Loire at Blois, had a hand in the erection of Ménars. In 1760 the house and its domaine were bought by the Marquise de Pompadour, who employed Gabriel to extend the house by a wing at each end. The result, though large (nineteen bays and three storeys), is a house that appears eminently habitable, and indeed it has been inhabited more or less continually until modern times. Only a few rooms are shown. They include an eighteenth-century kitchen with brick and stone quadripartite vaults, the vestibule with some interesting tapestries, and a pleasantly furnished music-room.

The park and gardens are the thing at Ménars. Laid out for Madame de Pompadour's brother, the Marquis de Marigny, who inherited the house in 1764, they are in the French style, geometrical and neat. They were designed by Soufflot, the architect of the Panthéon in Paris. There is nothing startling or extraordinary—a few follies such as a temple of love and a small grotto—but lawns and flowers and trees in plenty.

Beside the river, reached by a rocky little lane and outside the park, a footpath goes for about a mile among bushes beside the river. On sunny days people come here to picnic or to laze, and occasionally someone will bring a small flat-bottomed boat to go on the water. In summer the water is shallow, with the Loire creeping blue and limpid among yellow sandbanks.

Chaumont, some sixteen kilometres downstream from Blois, rises magnificently on a terrace high above the Loire. You climb to it up a steep, tree-shaded path and come to a massive gatehouse of whitish stone. It looks, with an air of conviction, like a medieval fortress of which the only condescension to comfort and later taste lies in the windows. Chaumont was indeed a medieval fortress, but its owner Pierre d'Amboise compromised himself in a rebellion against Louis XI, and the king destroyed the château. Pierre's son Charles began to rebuild about 1470, and the work went on after Charles's death. The new walls, however, including those of the imposing gateway, were made only six feet thick—ten or twelve feet would have been considered the minimum for defence; the walls of the château of Pierrefonds, a true military castle, are twenty feet thick. But if the walls are flimsy in a relative sense, the fortified gateway unable to repel a burglar, the machicolations and the *chemin de ronde* mere ornament, the whole thing is as pretty a piece of theatre as one could wish, and believable. One could not ask for a castle gatehouse more in accord with notions of what a romantic castle should be. One might say that it could have been built by Walt Disney, if that were not to put the cart before the horse. Even the drawbridge works, counter-balanced by two huge blocks of wood so that it may be opened and closed by a girl—as it is every morning and evening.

The decoration of the entrance towers and of the portal is interesting. Over the door, between the slots for the operation of the drawbridge, are the arms and the initials of Louis XII— Georges d'Amboise, admiral of France, was grand master of the house to Louis. In a panel on one of the flanking towers are the sculptured arms of Charles d'Amboise, and opposite to it the cardinal's hat of another member of the family. Around each tower is a frieze of panels, which carry alternately the interlaced Cs of Charles d'Amboise and a flaming mound, the '*chaud mont*'. The interlaced Cs served equally for a later owner, the widowed Catherine de Médicis, who bought the château in 1560 after the accidental death of her husband, Henri II, in a tournament in Paris. Catherine, it appears, acquired the château in a spirit of revenge. Her husband's mistress, Diane de Poitiers, had been given the more beautiful château of Chenonceau. Catherine compelled Diane to give up Chenonceau in exchange for Chaumont.

Diane did not care for Chaumont, and soon left it for Anet, but she put in hand the addition of the machicolations and the wall-walks under the pepperpot roofs of the towers, and there, on the machicolations, you may see her initial and the symbols of Diane the huntress.

Chaumont was built originally as a complete quadrangle. In the eighteenth century, long after the military security of a château had become a minor consideration, the north wing towards the river was removed, revealing a beautiful view down into the valley of the Loire.

The general effect of the courtyard contradicts the exterior of the château. Where that was gothic with touches of a later style, the courtyard is renaissance, with the older period showing in such details as crockets on the gables of the dormers and on pinnacles, cusped ornament on a balcony, and gothic buttresses to a tower, the rhomboid windows of which proclaim a staircase. The arcaded cloister *à la* Charles d'Orléans is seen here, too, with the double string-course above.

If Diane de Poitiers had removed the north wing to reveal the view of the Loire and the far distance beyond, instead of leaving it to a later generation, she might have stayed at Chaumont and found it pleasant enough, for, theatrical effects and all, it is really a delightful château; but perhaps she thought it too near to Chenonceau and to Catherine de Médicis. Madame de Staël, who was exiled from Paris by Napoleon because of her writings, and came to Chaumont, saw the view and did not think highly of it. She was a townswoman for whom the country had small attraction. She said she preferred the dirty little stream in the Rue du Bac in Paris rather than the Loire, whatever its beauty.

A little distance from the château are the stables, open to visitors. Lucky horses that dwelt in these unusual stables, safe and warm and pampered! In one corner rises a curious tapered structure under a roof like a Chinese hat (plate 12). It was originally a dove-house, and then became a workshop in which an Italian called Nini, financed by the owner of the château, made terracotta portrait medallions by the score. Later the circular interior proved an ideal *manège* for children, that is a place where they could be taught to ride and control a horse. Visitors to Chaumont should decidedly not miss the stables.

Touraine
Amboise to Candes

Touraine

On January 1790, in the revolutionary redrawing of boundaries that abolished the old princely provinces and created the modern *départements* of France, the royal province of Touraine became the *département* of Indre-et-Loire. It was a singularly inept and inefficient transformation. The name Indre-et-Loire, though logical enough, is without connotation, without antecedent, without romance. The name Touraine has all of these qualities, and in addition it comes more easily to the tongue. In a country in which changes of name are frequent and are dutifully accepted (if not always unanimously), Touraine has remained indomitably Touraine, as it does today. No one, except perhaps officials of local government or taxation, speaks of the *département* of Indre-et-Loire. Frenchmen and foreigners alike come to visit Touraine, to see the châteaux and the rivers and the countryside of Touraine, to drink the wines of Touraine, to meet the people of Touraine.

It is not a very large province and it is not heavily populated. It has only one considerable centre, the city of Tours, capital of the province for at least two thousand years from the time of its foundation by the Gallic tribe called Turones. Blois is nowhere near as large. Yet Touraine is more thickly sewn with fine châteaux than either of the other districts, the Orléanais and Anjou, that form the subject of this book. The reasons are not far to seek. Three good tributaries flow from the south into the Loire—the Cher, the Indre, and the Vienne—and make their contribution to a countryside that is pleasant to see and pleasant to live in. Châteaux and monasteries lie more thickly in this riverine country than they do north of the Loire, where tributaries are few and the country is upland plain, the Gâtinais, alternately woodland and cattle-raising land.

And then there is the wine. Touraine has famous vineyards that produce, as they have produced for many centuries, excellent wines of a surprising variety in so small an area, wines that range from the deep red of Bourgueil through a variety of rosés to the beautiful white wines of Vouvray and Montlouis. No connoisseur, no gourmet, no lover of good living could ask for better.

The wine comes from the soil, as it always does. The soil of the wine-land of Touraine is, much of it, chalk of the kind the French call *tuffeau*. It is obvious along the river banks, where it forms cliffs that have been pierced and excavated in a thousand places to form store-rooms, mushroom caves, and wine-cellars, and even cottages. The wines of the Loire valley of Touraine live as comfortably in the stable temperature of these caves as the troglodytes do in their hewn-out living-rooms.

It is no wonder that monks, dukes, and princes, and their mistresses chose to dwell in Touraine, no wonder that splendid mansions rose there to house them, no wonder that kings came here to relax or to hunt, or to retire and to die, as Louis XI did at Plessis-lès-Tours.

Chronologically, one should begin with the ruined château of Chinon, a defensive castle built by Henry II of England and Richard Cœur de Lion; all this country of Touraine, or much of it, was once part of the heritage of the throne of England. Henry, besides being King of England, was Duke of Normandy, Count of Anjou, and Duke of Aquitaine, and these were no mere empty titles—the country he ruled extended down to the Pyrénées, the whole of western France. Then one should move, still in the middle ages, to Loches, which was also a fortress of Henry II, and so to the thirteenth century at Luynes. Langeais marks the beginning of the end of the middle ages. After this comes a series of châteaux in which the Renaissance is more or less marked.

Such a route must mean a lot of toing and froing and expenditure of time, whatever its other advantages might be. So, as tourists, with limited time, we enter Touraine to begin with Amboise and proceed, as we have done with the Orléanais, downstream, with deviations to one side or the other to find châteaux and monasteries away from the main Loire valley.

5. Amboise to Montbazon

Coming from Chaumont along the south bank of the Loire, we enter Touraine at the village of Mosne. Borders seldom mark distinct divisions and there is nothing in the landscape or riverscape to announce that we have come into a different province. The province nevertheless has its own character, which is perceived with time and travel. The common factor is the Loire, with its green and yellow sand-ships reflecting in the blue water their masts and sails of tall trees and leafy branches.

The roads north and south along the river, the N152 and the less important N151, run near the water's edge, sometimes with views of the river and its islands to distract the motorist. The southern road leads to Amboise, the site of what was from the fifteenth century the largest renaissance château in the Loire valley. The château is not a ruin, but it is now much smaller than it used to be. What is left of it dominates from its height a town with many old streets that would preserve the air of centuries if it were not for that modern upstart the motor-car. Amboise is not a large town, but it is a busy one, and the rush of traffic and the French driver's *élan* fill it full of noise and movement. It has several industries, among which is the manufacture of fishing-rods.

There is a broad tree-bordered street along the river, the Quai Général de Gaulle, which becomes the Quai Charles Guinot where the high walls of the château look cheerfully down on the bridge over the Loire. The bridge, of many shallow arches, uses as a stepping-stone the long island of Saint-Jean,

once called the Île d'Or, on the prow of which a group of pop-
lar trees stands like a high forecastle. The island has a useful
camping-site. From the bridge or from the island you may have
a comprehensive view of the river front of the château, its pale
and fretted stone rising above the white-faced, slate-roofed
houses of the south bank. The château is built on a promontory
between the Loire and its small tributary the Amasse or La
Masse, a cliff carved by the river in ancient times. Clothed with
masonry, the cliff now has the appearance of a large and solid
wall, above which are seen the green trees of gardens within the
encircling fortification. What is seen of the château is the towers
and the walls of the *enceinte*, the ornate royal lodgings, and the
chapel of Saint-Hubert (or Saint-Blaise), the spire of which lies
to the right in this view from the north.

The site is an obvious one for a defensive work and in fact
there have been forts and fortifications here since prehistoric
times. When Charles vii confiscated Amboise from the Count
of Amboise there was a medieval château on the plateau.
Charles lived here in the days after his throne had been made
secure by the campaigns of Joan of Arc, whom he repaid with
ingratitude. Here too no doubt came the gentle Agnès Sorel,
the Dame de Beauté, who is better encountered at Charles's
other château of Loches.

Charles's son, also Charles, inherited as a minor under the
tutelage of his sister Anne de Beaujeu, who must have restrained
the lavish ambitions to which, as soon as he was able, he was to
give free rein. He had spent much of his boyhood at Amboise
with his mother Charlotte de Savoie. He now determined to
build a château of unrivalled size and splendour. With his new
wife Anne of Brittany he came to live at Amboise, where he
could watch the work and urge it forward. Despite its size—
the startled ambassador of Florence declared that Charles was
building a city—nothing should be allowed to delay completion, not even night or the weather. The king caused the workmen to work not only in the daytime but throughout the night
as well, by the light of torches, and throughout the cold of

winter also, when great fires were lit to warm the stones and the masons' hands. It was as though Charles had a premonition that his time was short and he wished to see the completion of the château. On the 7th of April 1498 he went to pass through a low doorway but struck his head on the lintel. An exclamation of annoyance, a rub or two, and he seemed to have come to no harm; but a short time afterwards he collapsed. Before the excited courtiers could decide what to do, he died. The consternation was such, with people running to and fro, that little thought was given to the corpse, which was allowed to lie neglected in a maladorous passage for hours; it is an illustration of the manners of the time that this passage could be described as a place where 'everybody pissed'.

Charles had made his mark, however, not only in the size of his château but in its style. It was he who returned from Italy with the Renaissance in his baggage, he who introduced the architects, the scholars, the painters and designers, the masons, and the gardeners of France to a new kind of thinking, a new way of seeing, a new way of living. Though the building of Amboise was interrupted by the death of Charles, the influence of the Renaissance spread. Louis XII carried it with the masons and the others from Amboise to Blois, where he began to remodel that château.

Amboise became the home of Louise de Savoie and of her two young children François and Marguerite—François, who was to become King of France, and Marguerite, the clever, good-looking girl who passionately loved art and literature, and herself wrote poetry (the *Marguerites de la marguerite des princesses*). Marguerite married first the Duc d'Alençon, and then in 1527 the King of Navarre. Under the careful eye of their mother the children spent an ideal childhood at Amboise. While Marguerite acquired the arts and ideals of womanhood, and adored her brother, François studied with scholars, learned to ride and to hunt in the extensive forest of Amboise, and constructed miniature castles, which he defended vigorously against his friends. He spent the first three years of his reign at Amboise, completing parts of the building and arranging balls, plays, tournaments, and other amusements. He brought notable men to the town, among them Leonardo da Vinci, to whom he gave a house, the manor of Clos-Lucé.

With Louis XII and François I the accent of gaiety passes to Blois. The last royal note in the story of Amboise is one of horror, the note of the Conjuration of Amboise. In 1560 the young François II was at Amboise with the Duc de Guise, when it was reported to them that one La Renaudie was leading a Protestant conspiracy against the Crown, to secure rights for the practice of their religion. It proved to be a plot of amazing naïveté and calamitous misfortune. It went wrong at every step. Its repeated failures gave or should have given ample warning to the conspirators to desist, but they persisted when they should have made themselves scarce and group by group they fell easily into the hands of the king's men or of Guise's men. The conspirators were put to death with frightful savagery, normal enough at that period; what marked this as particularly repellent was that the king and his court came after dinner to enjoy the spectacle. Among them was the queen, the young Marie Stuart, wife of François II, and better known to English history as Mary Queen of Scots. It is said she was sickened by the sight. The wretched conspirators were some of them hanged from the battlements, agonising almost within reach of the watching court at the windows; some were disembowelled and quartered, some decapitated, and some suffered all these punishments in sequence. There was blood everywhere, executioners waded in gore, and severed heads stood in dripping rows on the scaffolds.

Not everyone was as insensitive, as morally warped as the court of François II. The smell of blood seemed to be enough, to be sufficiently persistent, to exclude later kings from the château. Its most notable occupant, a century later, was Gaston d'Orléans one of whose many infidelities and rebellions caused the king, Louis XIII, to demolish the château's defences. Gaston had been given Amboise together with Blois.

Only a part of the enormous château conceived by Charles VIII and built by him and his successors remains today. The greater part was demolished by the Senate after the French Revolution. There is the circuit of the walls, with its defensive towers, and the two broad entrance towers of the Minimes and of Hurtault, one of which may be visited; there is the king's lodging, with an arcaded walk facing the Loire, tall first-floor windows above, and dormers with delicate spires and pinnacles—renaissance with undertones of gothic; and there is the chapel of Saint-Hubert perched on top of the wall above the narrow Rue Victor Hugo.

A few furnished rooms are shown in the king's lodging. The finest of these rooms is the Salle des États, a beautiful gothic chamber with a delicately rib-vaulted roof resting on a central row of pillars decorated with fleurs-de-lys and ermine tails in low relief—motifs that appear again thickly strewn on the hoods of two fine fireplaces. One cannot help feeling that it is a pity that a style that could achieve the purity of line and the splendour of this beautiful chamber should have passed away, never to be recaptured, not even by the most able medievalist architects of the gothic revival of the nineteenth century.

The chapel of Saint-Hubert, built in 1493, is also a masterpiece, of the more lavish kind the French call flamboyant; the design is derived from the Netherlands, exhibiting once again the breadth of the patronage and the eclecticism of Louis VIII. Stags' horns sprouting from the base of the spire symbolise the conversion of Hubert, who when hunting one day was moved to the Christian belief by the sight of a stag with a crucifix caught in its horns. The encounter appears deeply carved in a long panel over the door of the chapel (plate 13).

Above the panel, within the arch, the Virgin and Child sit within a mandorla, and kneeling one on either side are the figures of Louis XII and Anne de Bretagne. The whole piece is intricate, admirable, and moving even to the irreligious. Inside the building the clustering ribs of the roof bring the eye down to capitals and friezes crowded with finely detailed ornament carved in a stone of milk white tinged with cream. In the floor of the north transept a simple modern tomb-stone proclaims the burial place of the body of Leonardo da Vinci. Leonardo was originally interred in a larger church that also stood within the château, a church that has entirely disappeared. In the nineteenth century a search was made on the site for the grave of the artist. A tomb was found that contained a skull with a particularly noble brow. This, it was concluded, must be the skeleton of Leonardo, and it is this skeleton that now rests in the chapel of Saint-Hubert.

Leonardo lived at the manor of Clos-Lucé a few hundred yards from the château along the Rue Victor Hugo; the manor was then called Cloux. Clos-Lucé, completed in 1477, is built of red brick coigned with white stone. Charles VIII bought it in 1484, and François I offered it to Leonardo as a home. Leonardo came in May 1516, and died there three years later, in May 1519. François appears to have asked nothing of him in return for this hospitality; he simply wanted the celebrated but unfortunate old man to live his last years in peace. It is unlikely, however, that the mind of Leonardo could rest unemployed and among the things he *may* have done for François are designs for parts of the château of Chambord and for the staircase of Blois. The house is now a Leonardo museum. During the past few years it has been gradually restored to the state in which it was when Leonardo lived here, and has been furnished accordingly. The museum contains a number of models of mechanical devices built according to the sketches in Leonardo's notebooks, where they are described in his meticulous mirror-reversed script—the painter was completely left-handed even to the extent of writing backwards. The models include a parachute and a glider.

The picturesque D31 runs directly south from the town of Amboise through the Forêt d'Amboise, in which the Valois kings hunted the wild boar. Where a long straight forest ride, the Grande Allée, crosses the road, we turn right to find the pagoda of Chanteloup. This garden ornament is all that is left of the Duc de Choiseul's château of Chanteloup. The duke, one of the ministers of Louis xv, fell foul of Madame du Barry, who persuaded the king to exile him to his estate. There Choiseul passed his time by cultivating scholarship and the arts, bringing many notable men to stay at Chanteloup. He visited England and was so taken with the Chinese pagoda at Kew that he determined to have one of his own. Finished in 1778, it was the last splendour of the château of Chanteloup. The château afterwards became neglected and disused and in 1823 it was demolished for the value of its material.

It is always astonishing how much money, how much planning, and how much time spent in the construction of a château could by a later generation be held to be valueless and the château be demolished so that nothing or no more than a fragment remains. Chanteloup was by no means the only example. We have seen that the greater part of Amboise was knocked down for want of the will or of the money to maintain it. Other examples are Le Verger, Bury, Richelieu, Cinq-Mars. The larger the building, the more likely was it to be neglected for lack of funds.

The Duc de Choiseul could not have dreamed that his cherished château would vanish and nothing remain but his folly, his pagoda, on which he had set the inscription translated as follows: 'Etienne-François, Duc de Choiseul, sensible of the marks of friendship, of goodness, and of attention that he received during his exile, has built this monument to perpetuate his gratitude.'

The pagoda, reflected in the reedy pool by which it stands, has seven diminishing stages. You may climb to the top for a view of the Loire.

We continue southwards on the D31 and then east in search of the château of Chenonceau in the valley of the Cher. You will know already what this château looks like, for none in the Loire country has more often been painted, drawn, photographed. Every aspect of it is familiar as a picture postcard, and nothing indeed is more picturesque than this remarkable building rising from the unruffled waters of the Cher (plate 28).

It was originally the château des Houdes, set to one side of the river. Behind it a water-mill stood in the bed of the stream, with a bridge to the bank. It was the mill of the lord of the manor and his tenants would have been obliged to have their corn ground by the manorial mill-stones turning to the command of the current. The château was bought about 1513 by Thomas Bohier, intendant-general of finance to Louis XII. He put in hand a complete rebuilding. His work for the king and the wars in Italy called Bohier away from home for long periods, and in his absence the construction was overseen by his capable wife Catherine Briçonnet, whose retention of her maiden name seems to be a mark of the strength of her personality. The architect was probably the master-mason Pierre Nepveu, who is also known as Trinqueu, and to him we owe the beautiful house with round corner towers, *poivrière* roofs, and ornate dormers standing in the water by the north bank of the Cher. In its day it was an original, a novelty. The central doorway and the symmetrical front, with the rooms inside placed either side of a central hallway, express the Renaissance distinctly. As distinctive is the stairway, which for the first time was not spiral but ascended in two straight flights. Gothic persists in the pinnacles of the façade, in the round corner towers, and in the ribbed vaulting within the house—the entrance has a *tour de force* of vaulting, a curious zigzag central rib, a rare feature and one of small merit: it looks like the effort of a drunken mason, who must, however, have been sober enough to work out the complex lines of stress.

In 1526 the château was confiscated by the Crown and in 1547 Henri II gave it to his favourite Diane de Poitiers. A portrait of her by Primatice hangs in the castle. Twenty years older than the king, she kept his affection to the end of his life, to the exclusion of the queen, Catherine de Médicis. Primaticio's portrait is no doubt intended to flatter, but it does not show an amiable person. The face is of a classic beauty—alert eyes, slender, straight nose with lightly flared nostrils, perfect mouth —but the expression is hard and without sympathy and suggests a mercenary character.

After Henri's death Catherine became regent for her young son François II. The hitherto overshadowed queen showed an unexpected strength and determination in government and a revengeful spite that was understandable if not admirable. One of the first things she did was to turn Diane out of Chenonceau and compel her to accept Chaumont in exchange. Catherine herself took Chenonceau.

Diane had commissioned Philibert de l'Orme to build a bridge from the château to the south bank so that she could more easily reach the forests for hunting. Catherine now added a two-storey gallery on this bridge and so brought the château to the state in which it is seen today. The two parts of the building, that of Thomas and Catherine Bohier and that of Diane and Catherine de Médicis, are distinct, though linked by the charm of the situation and by the reflection in the water. Catherine's gallery, by the same architect as Diane's bridge, is a more severe, more classical structure, as a comparison of the pedimented dormers alone will show. It abuts on to the older house as though trying to elbow it aside.

Catherine also embellished the front of the main house with caryatids, pilasters, and other details that were not improvements. They remained until the nineteenth century.

Catherine's sickly son François II brought his wife Mary Queen of Scots to Chenonceau on occasions, and perhaps in this lovely place this ill-fated girl had some happiness. Henri III spent huge sums on receptions and fêtes and held transvestite parties in which the women of the court, naked to the waist, and in trunk hose, served courtiers garbed in women's attire. Louise de Lorraine, widow of the assassinated Henri III, mourned this unsatisfactory monarch by spending her days dressed in white in rooms hung all in black. The château fell on bad times in the eighteenth century until it was acquired by the *fermier-général* Dupin. There is a portrait of Dupin's wife in the château. Here is a face to contrast with that of Diane de Poitiers. Perhaps the most beautiful of the several ladies concerned with Chenonceau, Madame Dupin has an expression of friendliness, humanity, and charm. It was no flattery. She became in her long life—she lived in the château from 1733 to 1799—so popular with the people of the district that when the revolutionaries wanted to destroy the building they were persuaded to hold their hand—on the excuse that the house was the only bridge over the Cher for a considerable distance! Madame Dupin remained at Chenonceau through the worst days of the Revolution. Her successor, another woman, Madame Pelouse, removed Catherine de Médicis's doubtful decorations from the façade and restored the larger part of the château to its original state.

As we approach Chenonceau the isolated round Tour de Marques, named after the owners of the estate before the Bohiers, draws the eye. It is the sole remnant of the medieval gothic château, its keep, retained as the symbol of lordship or seigneury. The Bohiers had the windows of the tower changed to a renaissance design; these windows are the work of a competent architect, and the windows of the château itself seem to have been copied from them by a less able hand.

To the left of the forecourt in which the Tour de Marques stands is the garden of Diane de Poitiers, geometrical, *à la française*, which means *à la Renaissance*; without trees, it has sparse bushes trimmed to a conical shape, and colourful margins to green triangular beds that are embroidered with the swirls and curls of miniature box hedges.

Catherine de Médicis preferred a garden of her own and laid out one to the right of the forecourt, beyond a strip of water. Simpler in design, and smaller, it is equally geometrical.

Most of the rooms in the house are open and you may walk through them at your own pace. Many are furnished in appropriate style and contain tapestries of the fifteenth, sixteenth, and seventeenth centuries and paintings of diverse merit and value. The fireplaces are of interest, from that by the sculptor Jean

Goujon in Diane de Poitier's room to the ornate example in the drawing-room, decorated with the salamander of François I (who took the château from the heirs of the Bohiers), and the ermine tails of François's wife Claude de France. The chapel, facing upstream, is gothic, as may be seen inside and out, with a high interior and a wooden gallery used by the owners of the house to attend mass. The lower floor of the long gallery over the Cher is today one long room, with a black and white tiled floor. It was used as a hospital ward during the first world war and during the second as an escape route between German-occupied territory north of the river and the unoccupied zone to the south.

The town of Loches lies twenty-five kilometres to the south of Chenonceau, beyond the Forêt de Loches, through which the route D31 passes. In few places in the valley of the Loire does the atmosphere of the middle ages and the early Renaissance survive as it does in the streets and squares of Loches beneath the honey-coloured walls of the château and its *donjon*, which, with the church of Saint-Ours, stand on a long ridge that has been a natural fortress since men took to war. The ridge has been surrounded by a wall since at least the twelfth century, when Loches was part of the extensive dominions of Henry II of England. Loches was inherited by Richard the Lion-Heart and during Richard's imprisonment in Germany was traded by John in an agreement with Philippe-Auguste. On recovering his freedom the furious Richard came at once and retook the château in three hours, a feat that astounded the commanders of the time and filled the chroniclers with amazement. Philippe set out to recover Loches, but it took a year-long siege to do it.

Charles VII, at nearby Chinon, gave the château for the occupation of his mistress Agnès Sorel, a woman of great beauty whom he had found among the maids of honour of the court. As his mistress she exercised a strong influence, an influence largely for good. If Agnès had faults they included a love of luxury and a habit of baring her beautiful breasts and shoulders that was remarked with disapproval even in her own day—she liked to '*se descouvrait les epaules et le seing devant*', the chronicler Chastellain wrote. She appears in a fifteenth-century portrait in the château with one round breast protruding from her laced bodice; this picture is almost a copy of a painting of the Virgin and Child done by Jean Fouquet about 1450, for which Agnès sat. Because of these pictures we know exactly the appearance of Agnès Sorel, whom her contemporaries knew as the Dame de Beauté, giving to her in personal compliment the title of one of her châteaux near to Vincennes.

Louis XI used the château of Loches as a state prison, as which it soon gained a fearsome reputation, for the building stood over cellars and quarries carved out of solid rock—dark, dull, escape-proof chambers that served conveniently as oubliettes. For yet greater security or for more malicious revenge, some prisoners were kept by Louis XII in closely barred cages of iron-bound wood, from which some of the wretched men never emerged, even for bodily functions. Louis XII imprisoned at Loches the captured Duke of Milan, Ludovico il Moro—Ludovico who had been the friend and protector of Leonardo da Vinci during some of that artist's most productive years. True, Ludovico probably never paid Leonardo, but then he seldom paid his soldiers either, and that, when the French came to Milan, was his downfall. At Loches Ludovico was thrust into a cavern with a tunnel vault deep in the rock below the Martelet and there over a period of eight years he sought to keep his sanity by covering the walls and the curved roof with crude designs and sketches, including an attempt at a portrait of himself wearing a magnificent helmet, a memory of things past. He was released in 1508 and on climbing the steep stone stairs into the brilliance of the sun he fell down and died.

Beneath Ludovico's cell is another in which two bishops, of Autun and of Puy, who had taken part in a rebellion, scratched with their nails a little altar in the depth of the wall. Another prisoner was the Comte de Saint-Vallier, father of Diane de

Poitier; she pleaded for her father's life and succeeded in gaining for him the doubtful privilege of imprisonment in one of the *cachots* of Loches.

The buildings of Loches on their elevated ridge have remained little changed since the time of Louis XII. The wall enclosed not only the château, the *donjon*, and the church, but also a little town within itself. Another town grew up around it on the lower ground and in the sixteenth century this too was walled around. Nothing remains of these later walls but two important fortified gates, both at the north end, the Porte Picoys and the Porte des Cordeliers. The Tour Saint-Antoine (plate 19) is another survival from this period. These gates and the tower dominate the narrow little streets, and at this turning or that they spring up in one's face like exclamation marks. Attached to the Porte Picoys, the Hôtel de Ville interjects a renaissance note into the defensive gothic.

We enter the *enceinte* of the château by the Porte Royale and soon find ourselves facing the ponderous walls of the Église Saint-Ours. Saint Ours was a fifth-century saint of the district, whose name was given to the former collegiate church of Notre-Dame when it became the parish church in 1802. Dating largely from the twelfth century, built on an earlier crypt, the church is severely romanesque, with two large towers topped by short octagonal spires. Between the spires there appear, somewhat oddly, two more, squat, like pyramids. This latter pair cover the nave, the interior of which shows the hollow insides of these pyramids instead of vaults or domes. The ornate west door has fantastic animals and damaged figures of the Virgin and the three Magi.

The *donjon* at the southern end of the ridge, comprising the Tour Ronde, built in the fifteenth century, the *donjon* itself, eleventh-century and now floorless, but with a stair leading to the top, and the Martelet and its caves, in which so many prisoners spent so many dark days and months, is a part of the château that remains distinctly in the memory. Some of these underground chambers and passages, however, have never been prisons, but were simply quarries from which stone was drawn, and probably at times they were used as drains.

At the northern end of the ridge the château itself rears high above the town. We enter through the Tour Agnès Sorel and come on to a terrace bordered on one side by the royal lodging, built in two distinct periods. The nearer part, with half-round towers to the wall, is of the fourteenth century, the farther one, more distinctly renaissance, with its pinnacled dormer windows, is the work of Charles VIII and Louis XII.

While you wait on the terrace for the guide, take the opportunity to enjoy the view. The Tour Saint-Antoine springs up high from among the tumbled red roofs of the town, distinguished by its cupola. Left of it, with a clock, the Porte Picoys nudges the Hôtel de Ville. To the right the steeply pointed roof of the Porte des Cordeliers is flanked at the corners by the four drawn-out cones of its corner towers. Here and there among the roofs a pepperpot roof announces the survival of another detail of the thirteenth or fourteenth century.

Inside the *logis*, the visitor will not forget the oratory of Anne of Brittany, especially on a busy day. Your guide will crowd the whole of his party into this tiny room, scarcely more than ten feet square, and then lock the door in that inane fashion of Loire guides. You will scarcely be able to see that the walls of the oratory are covered all over with Anne's ermine tails, the symbol or emblem of her duchy of Brittany. In one corner stands a recessed stone altar on spiral columns, with a background of ermine tails among sinuous cords, the symbol of widowhood—at the time this oratory was built Anne was the widow of Charles VIII and had not yet become the wife of Louis XII.

In another room you will see a triptych painted in the fifteenth century by an artist working in the style of Jean Fouquet. It is one of several interesting pictures and tapestries in the château that are very worth attention. In the same room an alabaster figure of Agnès Sorel lies peacefully on a stone tomb-chest. The eyes are half-closed to slits, the mouth smiles slightly, the whole expression is that of a purring cat. Perhaps she is amused still by the egregious error of the revolutionaries who mistook the sinner for a saint and hacked the figure with their swords in a passion against superstition. Her hands are together in prayer and two angels peer at her face, while at her feet two lambs (*agneaux*) symbolise gentleness and pun the name Agnès. Agnès, who knew very well that she was a sinner in the eyes of the Church, gave large donations to the canons of Saint-Ours to ensure that she should be buried in that church; and so she was. Later the clerics repented and asked the king if they might eject the monument and the remains of such a sinner so unsuitably interred and put them in the château. You may, said the king, provided that the money she gave accompany the body. The clerics pressed the matter no further.

The older part of the château contains a sumptuous hall, in which two fine suits of armour emphasise the military aspect. Here in June 1429 Joan of Arc, who had already met and impressed the king at Chinon, met Charles VII again. The king was still uncrowned and Joan strove to persuade him to go at once to Reims and there to be crowned before all his nobles the true and only King of France.

Amateurs of ecclesiastical architecture may make an excursion eastwards from Loches, past the village of Beaulieu-lès-Loches— where the buildings of an abbey founded in 1004 by Foulques Nerra stand in ruins, with the abbey church intact as the parish church—along the N760 to the little round twelfth-century chapel of the Liget. The chapel, standing alone, is a puzzle, for no one knows why it was built in this particular place. It contains frescoes of the twelfth century. In order to get in to see them you will need to get the key at the Chartreuse du Liget farther along the N760. This monastery was founded by Henry II of England in expiation of the murder of Thomas Becket, a murder that seemed so opportune in the heat of the moment but turned out to be an expensive mistake. The

monastery was entirely rebuilt in classical style from 1787 onwards. It has a gateway of unusual beauty.

You may reach Tours from Loches most quickly by taking the
N143, the main road, but you will have greater pleasure if you
turn off at Chambourg-sur-Indre to follow the D17 beside the
winding river Indre to Cormery, and then along the D17 and
the Indre valley once more to Montbazon. Here at Montbazon
Foulques Nerra erected a large rectangular keep, during one of
his many quarrels with the counts of Blois. Today the keep is a
ruin, as are many other similar keeps. What distinguishes this
one is that in 1866 someone thought the highest part of the ruin,
the north-east corner, was a suitable place for an enormous
bronze statue of the Virgin. The figure stands perched there in
what seems to be a very precarious position, a monument to the
bizarre notions that on occasion afflict man.

The broad N10 leads directly into Tours, to become the Rue
Nationale, which goes straight past the Place Jean-Jaurès to
the Pont Wilson over the Loire.

6. Tours

Tours is not the largest of the three cities along the length of the Loire valley between Gien and Angers, but it has the air of a metropolis and it is busily expanding north and south with modern high-rise blocks and planned estates for housing and industry. It is a very ancient place—before the coming of the Romans it was a capital of the Gaulish tribe of the Turones, and for the Romans themselves, who called it Caesarodunum, it was a place of importance. Saint Martin was the apostle of Christianity here in the fourth century, and Gregory of Tours, its bishop, wrote a history of the Franks in the monastery he founded in the sixth century—he originally came to Tours to be cured of an illness at the tomb of Saint Martin. Today Tours is an industrial centre, a market for the wines, cattle, and other produce of the district, and an important shopping centre whose main shopping street, the Rue Nationale, would do credit to a national capital.

Crossing this main thoroughfare at the Place Jean-Jaurès is a broad boulevard divided by a long central island shaded by rows of old elm trees and chestnuts; to the west of the Place Jean-Jaurès this is the Boulevard Béranger, to the east the Boulevard Heurteloup. You may park your car on these boulevards, beneath the trees.

The older part of Tours lies north of the boulevards, between them and the Loire. In the midst of the city, miraculously preserved, the former garden of the eighteenth-century convent of the Visitandines remains green and colourful with trees and flowers and reflects in its little pond the convent's colonnaded and pedimented façade. The building is now the préfecture of the *département* of Indre-et-Loire. Behind it, to the north-east, the cathedral of Saint-Gatien flings two flamboyant towers high into the sky, their tops decorated each with a renaissance 'crown'. The building of this cathedral was begun in the thirteenth century and went on to the sixteenth. Here, as at Orléans, the builders, with archaeological interest, worked on in the developing gothic style, so that from east to west, from simple early gothic to the intricacy and multiple images and shadows of the flamboyant, the cathedral is an object lesson in the development of the mind and of the style of the medieval mason—with just that renaissance note on the tower tops to mark the end of his period.

The west front is one of those marvellous compositions of high gothic in which almost every stone contributes a detail of ornament, of light and shadow, to a total effect that gladdens the heart and gives the eye no rest from excitement. One looks at it with a glance that moves and roves and climbs from the rich arches of the three doorways, past their fretted hoods to lacy roundels and rose windows, and then by crocketed gable and soaring buttresses to the polygonal stages beneath the renaissance crowns.

The interior of the cathedral is interesting mostly for the ancient glass, through which the suns of six hundred years have driven their beams to spread pools of colour on the stone floors and on the walls. The windows of the ambulatory chapels and of the choir were made in the thirteenth century, the two splendid rose windows of the transepts in the fourteenth century, and the west window in the fifteenth century. At certain times of the year the light penetrates into a chapel of the south transept to colour the recumbent figures of two of the children of Charles VIII and of Anne of Brittany, who died in infancy. Carefully sculpted by Guillaume Regnault, with the symbols of royalty on their coverlets, the figures lie between kneeling angels at head and foot on a richly renaissance tomb-chest by the Italian sculptor Jerome de Fiesole.

South of the cathedral the former palace of the archbishop, built in the seventeenth and eighteenth centuries, is now the museum of fine arts. It looks on to a courtyard almost filled by a magnificent cedar planted in 1804. In one of the stables facing the tree another giant, a stuffed elephant left by Barnum and Bailey's circus, stands amid an assembly of odd pieces of stone.

North of the cathedral the cloister of the Psallette is half concealed behind enormous ornamented piers from which two tiers of flying arcs curve parabolically to the walls of the church (plate 21). The cloister is richly flamboyant, with a handsome open stair-tower of 1524 leading to the chapter-house.

Farther north the Tour de Guise, machicolated and military and standing within the enclosure of a barracks, is all that remains of the medieval château of Tours, built in the twelfth century by Henry II of England to defend the bridge. The present bridge, the eighteenth-century Pont Wilson, lower downstream than the medieval one, crosses a river that, even for the Loire, is exceptionally littered with islands, islands populated by rows of trees and with the yellow of the silted sand showing through the grass in the typical Loire manner.

We return a few steps to take the Rue Colbert westwards, and a short distance along this come to the Place Foire-le-Roi, beside which rise fifteenth-century houses with the kind of closely spaced diagonal timbering, forming lozenges filled with brick, that is to be seen in several streets of old Tours (plate 20), and yet again in Angers. The narrow, irregular streets around this square are a survival of the medieval plan. A few steps farther brings us to the Rue Nationale and almost on the corner stands the church of Saint-Julien. The west tower is fine romanesque of the twelfth century, with good capitals. The church itself is for the greater part late gothic. The church is a centre for the *compagnonnages*, the companies of wine-makers or *vignerons*, of Touraine, and a sixteenth-century wine-press stands in the centre of the ancient cloister garth north of the church. One side of the cloister has a very beautiful medieval cellar, opening by arcades to the cloister garth, and divided down the middle by slender columns supporting a ribbed roof. Wine-tastings take place here in surroundings that must enhance the flavour of the wine.

Cross the busy Rue Nationale into the Rue du Commerce, past the ebullient front of the Hôtel Gouin, whose early renaissance façade survived bombs and burning during the war. The house is now the museum of medieval and renaissance art of the Société Archéologique de Touraine. It exemplifies the luxury in which a rich merchant of the early sixteenth century lived, and the love of decoration typical of the period, which was expressed in dress, in hangings, and in every aspect of the life of the more wealthy citizens.

The Rue du Commerce leads into the Place Plumereau, and we are in the midst of the oldest part of the city, where the streets are narrow and more closely spaced, and street names reveal the trades that once went on in the shops and booths. The Place Plumereau was once a market for hats, the Carroi aux Chapeaux, and if the present name is only accidentally appropriate, it will do. The Rue du Commerce, the Rue du Change, and the Rue de la Monnaie reveal the overriding interest of the dealers who once traded here, and so do the Rue de la Rôtisserie and the Rue des Orfèvres. Timber-frame houses with lozenges of bricks and carved wood corner posts nod over the *place*, and there are more in the side streets (plate 20). Some of them are distinguished by rows of overlapping slates following and covering the timbers. A house just off the *place*, in the Rue du Change, has on its corner-post a beautiful but unfortunately mutilated carving, a figure of the Virgin with a headless Child on her knee and a handless Saint Joseph beside her (plate 27). It is full of the tenderness attributed to the Virgin and notably absent in the painting by Jean Fouquet for which Agnès Sorel sat (see page 91).

We pass down the Rue du Change and turn left into the Rue du Châteauneuf, which brings us to the Place du Châteauneuf and the Tour Charlemagne. This huge tower was one of the transept towers of the immense basilica of Saint-Martin. The basilica, founded by Saint Martin in the fifth century, was rebuilt in the eleventh to thirteenth centuries, destroyed by the Huguenots in 1562, and finally demolished in 1802, when the present Rue des Halles was built through the length of the site of the former nave and the Rue Descartes straight across the transepts. The grave of Saint Martin, which was in the centre of the sanctuary, is preserved in its original position in the modern and somewhat monolithic church of Saint-Martin, which you see opposite the Tour Charlemagne. Part of the cloister of the old Saint-Martin survives in a convent in the Rue Descartes, and may be visited on request. Farther down the Rue des Halles the Tour de l'Horloge remains, the southern of the two west towers of the medieval basilica.

There are many picturesque old corners and alleys in Tours, and it is worth while, if you have the time, to wander about with open eye and ready camera. But if you wish to return to where you started I suggest that you go east along the Rue des Halles to cross the Rue Nationale into the Rue de la Scellerie. This long, narrow street, with its insufficient pavements often blocked by discharging or loading vans, was in the middle ages the street of saddlers. Its houses are a medley of periods, some very old, with their ground floors turned into narrow and very varied shops. Whatever oddity you may require, whatever strange or specialised object you need, I daresay you may find it here, between the little cafés and pâtisseries, the laiteries and boulangeries. Window-shopping in the Rue de la Scellerie is fascinating. But look at the buildings too. Here and there an architectural survival may be noticed, as for example the blocked fourteenth-century arched doorway in the side wall of a nineteenth-century theatre built on the site of a monastery.

The priory of Saint-Cosme or Saint-Côme lies to the west of the city, on the edge of the built-up area—neither townscape nor countryside and as depressing as such intermediate places

20. Timber-framed houses in Tours (*see* plate 27)

21. (*Left*) Buttresses of the cathedral of Tours. Behind them the cloister of the Psallette

22. (*Above*) Fifteenth-century tower arch of the priory of Saint-Côme, where the poet Ronsard was prior

23. (*Below*) The romanesque sanctuary of Saint-Côme

24. The château of Saché, where Balzac wrote

25. Ussé, the castle of the Sleeping Beauty

usually are. The priory itself is delightful even in ruin. Built in the eleventh and twelfth centuries, and altered up to the fifteenth century, when the nave of the church was rebuilt, and the seventeenth century, when the ancient prior's house was rearranged, the priory was set beside the Loire with that perceptive eye for situation and effect that monks so often have shown. Of the fifteenth-century nave little more than one of the crossing arches survives (plate 22), of the east end just the ambulatory and its radiating chapels, in the robust romanesque of the eleventh century (plate 23). The ruins are neatly maintained by the municipality of Tours.

What makes Saint-Côme of particular interest is that the priory was the home of Pierre Ronsard. Ronsard was appointed *prieure commendataire* in 1565 and held this office until he died in the prior's house in 1585. It was a kind of sinecure, granted to give him an income, but not weighing heavily on his time and energy. It meant his taking holy orders of a kind, and the corollary of this was that he was not allowed to marry. Perhaps this was an advantage for a philanderer such as the poet was, for this man, who appears so poetically ascetic in the bust you may see in the prior's house at Saint-Côme (though there is the hint of a smile on the lips), was passionately fond of girls, especially of young girls of fifteen or sixteen—Cassandre, Marie the Angevine, Hélène de Surgères. Girls matured early in that time and were already young women in their mid teens. Ronsard was no lecher—in most cases, perhaps in all, his passion was platonic, poetical. He admired the girls' bright eyes, their glossy hair, their beautiful figures, and made their charms subjects for his verse. There is no love poet in French the equal of Ronsard, none writing so directly in language very near to normal speech, a language his untutored girls could understand, though the poems were not written *for* them in that sense. He wrote:

> *J'aime à faire l'amour, j'aime à parler aux femmes,*
> *A mettre par écrit mes amoureuses flammes,*

J'aime le bal, la danse, et les masques aussi,
La musique et le luth ennemi du souci.

(I like to make love, I like to talk with women,
to express in writing my amorous fire,
I like the ball, the danse, and the masque also
and music and the luth, enemy of care.)

On a cold spring day of 1560 Ronsard with a friend, Jean-Antoine, coming from La Possonière, the poet's home, descended on a Saint-Côme all in festival for a wedding, with crowds of celebrators and dancers everywhere. They went in search of girls and each found an old flame. Ronsard's was Marie the Angevine, whom he had last seen years before. She had grown from the grace of her mid-teens into a sturdy village woman. Under the eye of a watchful mother Ronsard and Marie spent an innocent afternoon. The poet could be cruel, however:

Les garcons du village
Disent que ta beauté tire déjà sur l'age.

(The boys of the village
say that already your beauty tends to age.)

The word 'lès' or 'lez' in Plessis-lès-Tours means 'near'; the name means 'the fortress near Tours'. Plessis-lès-Tours was one of the favourite châteaux of Charles VII and especially of his son Louis XI, who spent the last few years of his life here and died in the château on the 30th of August 1483. It originally had three wings on a U plan, the arcaded lodging of the king facing the open side. It was not large, as châteaux go—the king's lodging had a façade of thirteen bays—and it was distinctly a house and never the sinister and terrible feudal castle that Sir Walter Scott, who evidently never saw it, supposed it to have been in one of his novels. It was built of brick coigned with stone. Today all that is left is half of the king's lodging and the stair tower serving it. The building is now a museum, of interest in particular for the Tourangelle silk industry, which was founded and encouraged by Louis XI and flourished in Tours for many years. Here, perhaps, one may catch something of the spirit and personality of Louis XI, that excessively ugly king—his portraits show him with an enormous knobbly nose overhanging a short upper lip—who by means of subtlety, unscrupulousness, and a naked exercise of power, together with a penchant for economy that was seen as meanness, lifted France from the difficulties of the aftermath of the Hundred Years War.

About eight kilometres east of Tours are the vineyards of Vouvray and Montlouis—Vouvray north of the Loire and Montlouis to the south of it. Here you will find the home country of the best white wines of the Loire valley. Yet these wines are not consistent. So far to the north of the richest wine country the sun is not dependable, and so in one year the wines of Vouvray and Montlouis may be good, in the next year excellent. The best years keep remarkably well for a white wine and it may take ten years in bottle for such a wine to arrive at its perfection. But do not let that deter you from drinking the previous year's vintage. Nowadays much Vouvray is blended to maintain a more even quality. It is an exceedingly refreshing wine, with a slight flavour of quinces and a little of their astringent liveliness on the tongue—yet Vouvray is typically sweet or slightly sweet, as in fact are most of the Loire wines. If you would have the unblended wine of Vouvray look for the labels of Marc Brédif and of Gaston Huet.

Vouvray is in chalk country and the grape, the Chenin blanc, grows on a chalky soil on an upland that ends in low cliffs towards the river. These cliffs are honeycombed with caves, some of which are the homes of the vineyard workers; others—some of great extent—are where the wine is stored. You may visit several of these caves and taste the product.

Montlouis requires a separate journey, for there is no bridge over the Loire between Tours and Amboise. The little town is on a steep-sided hill, clustered about its modest square and its church. The wine is similar to that of Vouvray—if you can distinguish it from Vouvray without difficulty then you have naturally a very good nose and palate for wine and ought to be a connoisseur. It is generally agreed, however, that Montlouis is not the equal of Vouvray and does not improve as long in the bottle.

Vouvray and Montlouis go excellently with fish or salad, but they are also wines that may be drunk alone, slightly chilled—very refreshing on a hot day.

7. Luynes to Villandry

We take the road west along the north bank of the Loire, a road divided from the river by an embankment and subject to fresh winds that blow from the immense wooded spaces to the north (in which you may drive for miles without encountering anything larger than a hamlet). We turn off the main road at Vallières, to take a lesser road that runs in a valley or hollow parallel with the main road. I suggest this road simply because it is not a main road, because it is narrow in places, with occasional difficult corners that will slow you down, and because it has more interest. Along this road you will see, perhaps for the first time, the famous troglodyte houses of the Loire valley.

Some of these may not be obvious at first sight for what they are. The caves have been fronted with masonry, but look carefully and you will see that the part standing clear of the cliff may not be deep enough to be of use to anyone, is simply a façade. Some other examples are more patently caves, higher in the cliff face and reached by steep little meandering paths. But they are a long way from the caves of primitive tribes. The cave opening is provided with rectangular, properly made doors and windows, which, wherever there is space, look out on to colourful little sloping gardens. If you were to go into one of these cave-houses you would find that three walls of a room are solid rock. In perhaps most instances this might not be obvious, for the room is as square as any built by a mason; but in others a bulge or irregularity of stone too hard to cut has been left as it is and then you see that this is indeed a cave.

The road comes suddenly into the market square of Luynes. This name is one of those that appear to give trouble to foreigners and in particular to English visitors. It should be pronounced *Loo-een*. The place was called Maille until 1619, when the château was bought by the Connétable de Luynes. The constable was created a duke and the village took the name of Luynes in his honour. The duke's castle still stands atop a cliff, dominating the village and the land around for miles, a very romantic sight. What you see is of the thirteenth century, and strictly a military fortress, except for the windows that at various periods have been cut into the thick walls in place of the medieval slots and loops—for the castle is lived in. It has been inhabited constantly since 1619 by descendants of the first Duke of Luynes. The present duke does not care, it seems, to have visitors, or need them, and as Michelin says, *on ne visite pas*. In other words, you cannot get in.

The château is still a rectangle of four wings, presenting a fortified face on each side. The courtyard contains later buildings, whose construction of brick and stone was undoubtedly inspired by Plessis-lès-Tours.

The château stands on the point of a plateau. Two faces of the building look vertically down on the town, another looks over the plateau where long straight rows of vines hang on wires.

Because the château cannot be visited, and there is nothing else of sufficient interest to draw visitors in large numbers—not even the ruins of a Gallo-Roman aqueduct of the fourth century —Luynes remains a small and truly French town. For me that is its charm. The wood-framed market hall dates from the fifteenth century. Here and there an old house preserves some antique features. The Hôtel de la Halle is there to serve the locals and the farmers who come in to buy and sell agricultural produce. The hotel will not by any means turn you away if it has room, but you must eat as the locals do. And you will eat well. Here I was given a lesson by the young Madame Neveu, wife of the proprietor (who is the chef), on how to eat *rillettes de Touraine*—generously applied to a morsel of crusty bread and washed down with *vin ordinaire*—or better, with the deep red Bourgueil.

We take the road west from the square and emerge on to the N152, the riverside main road, at Pont-de-Bresme. In about four kilometres we come to the ruined château of Cinq-Mars-la-Pile. 'La pile' is a Roman tower of uncertain purpose, which stands near the village. It has little to do with the château. The best known owner of the château, the Marquis de Cinq-Mars, born in 1620, was a handsome, even pretty young man who was selected by Cardinal Richelieu to be the favourite of Louis XIII. Henri de Cinq-Mars found his time at court excessively tiresome and the rigid control of Richelieu unbearable. He chose to rebel, invited the help of Spain, and was found out. At the age of twenty-two he was executed. Alfred de Vigny wrote a novel about Cinq-Mars's life and there is an opera by Poisson and Gallet, set to music by Gounod.

The château was destroyed by order of Richelieu. Three hoary towers and the remains of a fourth are still to be seen. They show that the château was a medieval castle.

Five kilometres west of Cinq-Mars we come into the town of Langeais, where the item of principal interest makes itself obvious. It is the château, which rises monstrous and military directly from the street.

There has been a château here since the tenth century, built by Foulques Nerra during his frequent wars with the Count of Blois. Its keep, huge, square, and ruinous, still stands on its motte behind the later château, contrasting the military bluntness and discomfort of the tenth century with the more subtly engineered defences of the fourteenth. The need for a new château seemed to Louis XI at the time of the revolt of the Ligue du Bien publique to be sufficiently strong to warrant the expenditure of a great deal of money. He chose Jean Bourré, his faithful minister, to design it for him. Jean Bourré was a genius in the art of fortification and in the defences of Langeais his mind may be seen at work. Heavy machicolations under a covered *chemin de ronde* ran all round the exterior walls, or rather were planned to, for the château was never completed. Two formidable towers flank the entrance facing the street, with their upper parts, under pepperpot roofs, set back. Between the towers, the gate still has the projecting wooden beams by means of which the drawbridge was raised. The exterior of the building, towards the town, is all severity and fortification and remarkably consistent. This consistency is attributable to the fact that the château was built quickly, in the years between 1465 and 1469. Even so, it was overtaken by time, by developments in politics and the art of war, and the full rectangular plan that was intended was never achieved. If it had been, Langeais would undoubtedly have been the finest specimen of a military château in the Loire valley. Two wings only, on an L plan, were completed.

The courtyard elevation is less deterrent than is the exterior. Langeais, after the example of Plessis-Bourré, was intended to be a habitable house as well as a military castle, and the courtyard elevation shows that this was the case. Its ranges of windows and dormers, the stair-towers, the absence of fortifications all proclaim it. It is all gothic. The Renaissance, even at this date, scarcely appears. But inside the château the planning and apportionment of the rooms suggests something other than a barrack protected by strong stone walls. This was a house that would have been furnished much as it is today—for Langeais is furnished in an appropriate style, enlivened by pictures of the period and by a series of medieval tapestries. The furniture, the pictures, and the tapestries were collected by the last owner of the château, Jacques Siegfried, who, bless him, gave it all to the Institut de France in 1904.

Langeais is one of the many satisfying châteaux of which a great deal is shown to the public—though under the tutelage of a guide. You may even climb to the tops of the towers and squeeze along the narrow, enclosed wall-walk, with the apertures of the machicolations at your feet, and look down from the archers' rectangular openings to the junction of streets below, down on to the steep-slated roofs, the gables and the dormers, and down on to a café that claims to be one of the houses frequented by Rabelais—who was, of course, a man of the Loire country.

In the Salle d'Honneur in December 1491 Charles VIII of France married Anne, Duchess of Brittany. On that cold day so near Christmas a great fire would have burned in the wide fireplace as the pomp of the ceremony proceeded, as the slim young king with the thin Valois nose and alert eyes placed his ring on the finger of the plump, gentle Anne, Anne of the round face with thinly pencilled, arched eyebrows and simpering mouth. Brittany was practically an independent duchy and by accepting the wedding-ring from Charles Anne united her duchy to the Crown of France. That, indeed, was the purpose of the marriage. France and Brittany were to descend together to the heirs of the Valois. But Anne's children died and lie in the cathedral of Tours, and Charles himself died inopportunely from knocking his head against that low beam at Amboise. In the middle ages a duchy belonged personally to its duke or its duchess, and Anne now found herself and her duchy free again. Charles's successor, Louis XII, married the widowed Anne to ensure that Brittany should remain with the Crown of France.

Langeais, of the grim, warlike stance, was the last of the medieval military castles of the Loire. Time and events moved quickly, and men's minds were changing, changing even before the full force of the renaissance mode and renaissance thought struck them. Langeais was early out of date, inadequate. It was almost contemporary with the unfortified Plessis-lès-Tours, and only a generation before the building of the Louis XII wing at Blois. Between Langeais and Blois lie the Renaissance and a more settled government in France.

We take the main road west out of Langeais, beside the Loire, and turn off after eight kilometres on to the D35 for Bourgueil, not because the architecture of this place is of deep interest (though there is a sixteenth- to seventeenth-century abbey you may visit), but in order to tip our hats and raise our right arms for the best red wine of the Loire. The grape from which it is made, the Cabernet franc (the Breton), grows in vineyards around the villages of Bourgueil and Restigné. Spend your money on a bottle of the previous year's vintage or of one three or four years old and drink this deep red wine with red meat or a strongly flavoured dish such as *coq au vin* or game.

Red wine is made in various places between Bourgueil and Chinon, to which we come next.

We take the N749 south to cross the Loire where the great silver ball of a nuclear power station shines from the south bank. Vineyards run parallel with the river on this bank, and then at the village of Avoine we enter the large area of vine country that extends all the way to Chinon and far beyond, along the river Vienne.

The quays beside the river in Chinon, the Quai Charles VII and the Quai Jeanne d'Arc, commemorate in their names the two best-known persons in the story of Chinon, but the quays themselves, with their busy shops, hotels, and cafés, are more reminiscent of any French boulevard than they are of old Chinon. Along the length of these quays on the edge of the water, until the nineteenth century, rose the town walls, with a towered gatehouse at the entrance to the bridge built by Henry II of England. At the western end, where the walls turned north and began to climb, the Tour Billard marked the angle. The base of this tower, projecting towards the river, was chosen as the site for a monument to the Resistance of 1940–44.

Turn any corner north from the quays and you will find yourself climbing steeply between ancient houses towards the oldest part of the town and the château. The château you can scarcely miss. It stands atop a long cliff and everywhere you turn your eyes up to that cliff there are fortified walls of a bright white stone that dazzle in the sunshine. As with so many military châteaux, the site is an obvious place, to be seized upon by the first imaginative brigand looking for a lair. There were fortifications here in prehistoric times, and the Romans had some kind of building on the cliff, remnants of which are built into a wall within the *enceinte*. In the tenth century the château belonged to Thibault, Count of Blois. In 1044 it was acquired by Geoffrey Martel, Count of Anjou, and from him it descended to the Angevin or Plantagenet counts who in the person of Henry II inherited the throne of England. Henry lived most of his life in his French possessions, and resided for long periods at Chinon. He rebuilt much of the château and added the Fort Saint-Georges at the east end. He also built the stone bridge over the Vienne, some parts of which remain from his time. Henry died in the château in 1199, a man saddened by the murder of Thomas Becket in Canterbury (if not by his orders, then by a rash exclamation taken too literally by his murderous knights), and by the rebellion of his sons and their mother. His body was carried in state to be interred in the abbey of Font-evraud a few kilometres to the north-west.

Henry's son Richard, the Cœur de Lion, quitted Chinon to go on crusade, and on his return found himself compelled to fight for his French domains. Mortally wounded at the siege of Chalus, he was brought back dying to Chinon in 1199; he is said to have breathed his last either in the château or in a house that still stands in the old town below the walls. He too was carried to Fontevraud.

King John, the bad King John of English romantic history, certainly neglected to defend his French possessions and Philippe-Auguste saw an opportunity to capture Chinon; but it took him nearly a year of siege to take the château. After-wards Chinon was the temporary home of French kings and queens, and was at times a prison—the principal members of the Order of the Templars, with their grand master Jacques de Molay, framed and brow-beaten into false confessions, which they later retracted, were incarcerated here until the stake and the fire were prepared for them in Paris.

The Dauphin Charles, who was to become Charles VII, made Chinon the centre of that part of France that was left to him by his enemies the English and by the Duke of Burgundy. Here he held his court, the glum, refugee court of a man who doubted the legitimacy of his birth and consequently whether he was truly the Dauphin of France, or, when his father died in 1422, the rightful King of France. Charles whiled away his time with the jejune ceremonies and pastimes of court life, with his wife Marie of Anjou, and with his beautiful mistress Agnès Sorel, whom he placed in a house outside the château walls, with discreet access by a tunnel. Agnès, the first of the recognised mistresses of a French king (a line that was to include Gabriel d'Estrées, Madame du Barry, and the Marquise de Pompadour), bore Charles several children.

On the 8th of March 1429 Charles was visited in his château by an eighteen-year-old peasant girl from Domrémy who, absurdly, wanted him to put her at the head of an army to relieve the city of Orléans, then besieged by the English. In order to test her Charles played the childish trick of hiding himself among the three hundred courtiers in the hall, but Joan, of course, recognised him at once. It was perhaps not as wonderful as it seems. His years of powerlessness and tutelage had imprinted on Charles's face an expression of sullen weariness that he was never to lose. Those long, sad features, and his slipshod mode of dress, were sufficiently well known, would have marked him out. The trick, none the less, had a profound effect on Charles, and convinced him that Jeanne d'Arc was truly a girl sent from God. She said so herself. 'Gentil Dauphin, j'ai nom Jehanne la Pucelle, et vous mande le Roy des Cieux par moi que vous serez sacré et couronné dans la ville de Reims, et serez le lieutenant du Roy des Cieux qui est le Roy de France' —'Gentle Dauphin, my name is Joan the Maid, and the God of Heaven tells you by me that you shall be consecrated and crowned in the town of Reims, and shall be the lieutenant of the God of Heaven, who is the King of France!' Then she reassured him of the legitimacy of his birth and so of his title to the throne of France.

The court and the government of Charles VII remained at Chinon until the year 1450. Chinon may be said with reason to have been the beginning of the long association of the kings of France with the valley of the Loire, the association that gave rise to the series of fine châteaux for which the valley is today famous.

After this time the château of Chinon was only occasionally visited by the court and the kings. As Langeais was, it was too much of a castle, without the grace of the Renaissance; but Louis xi, Charles viii, and Louis xii all came for longer or shorter periods. In 1498 Louis xii held court at Chinon and was visited by no less a person than Cesare Borgia, who came in the guise of a legate from his father Pope Alexander vi. Cesare brought with him the papal bull that allowed Louis to divorce his wife Jeanne de France and to marry instead Anne of Brittany. Jeanne limped from a malady of the hip, she was hump-backed, and her face was said to be simian; but she was the daughter of Louis xi and for reasons of state Louis xii at the age of fourteen had been compelled to accept her as his wife. No one asserts that this unfortunate girl was not intelligent, and now she had to watch helplessly while her husband deserted her and chose another woman. As soon as Louis became king and his own master he had set the divorce in motion.

In the seventeenth century the château became the property of Cardinal Richelieu, who demolished parts of it for the sake of the stone, which he transported to his new town and château of Richelieu—the cardinal was in process of creating a new town that he hoped might become the capital of France; it failed to do so. The family of Richelieu held the château of Chinon until the Revolution, and allowed much of it to fall down.

The château is a ruin that yet speaks eloquently of its former glory. It is three châteaux in one. To the east is the Fort Saint-Georges, built by Henry ii of England to protect the entrance to the Château du Milieu, from which it is divided by a deep dry moat. To enter the Château du Milieu you cross this moat by a stone bridge where once a drawbridge worked and pass through a gateway in the foot of a remarkable tower, the Tour de l'Horloge. Tall and very narrow, with one rounded side, it is like nothing more than a book standing on edge, as in a bookcase; it houses a small museum concerning Joan of Arc. Straight ahead you come to a circular space, a junction of paths beneath a large tree. From here you have a view of the roofless interior of what was the principal hall of the château. On the far wall hangs a fine gothic fireplace, which shows the level of the former floor. It was to this hall that Joan came on that day in 1429, climbing the steps to the entrance, and then crossing the long floor to recognise the Dauphin at once. Beyond the hall are the royal quarters, which are now roofed and restored but empty. From the windows there are extensive downward views of the narrow streets and steep roofs of the old town, and beyond of the bridge crossing the Vienne. Beyond the river there is a caravan and camping-site beneath young trees, next to public swimming pools.

The royal quarters of the Château du Milieu border on the west side on a deep dry moat that crosses from the southern to the northern walls of the enclosure. The part beyond the moat is the Fort du Coudray, the principal building of which is the *donjon* du Coudray, a fat, circular tower with thick walls, the principal keep of the castle. It has three storeys. Joan of Arc inhabited the middle floor for a month while learned doctors and divines debated whether she came from God or from the Devil and the Dauphin Charles, already believing in her, bit his lip and twiddled his fingers with impatience. The learned men, unable to decide so important a matter, sent Joan to Poitiers, where she had to go through it all again before it was decided that she might be trusted to do the king no harm and she could be allowed to return to Chinon.

The uppermost chamber of the tower was at some time turned into a pigeon-house.

There is little more to the château of Chinon. It is pleasant to look through the various windows to see the views, and pleasant to walk along the ramparts on the north side above the fields of growing vines, the Breton grapes that produce the soft red wine of Chinon.

We descend—if that is a polite word for an almost headlong tumble—to the old town either by the long stairway of the Rue de la Brèche into the Place de l'Hôtel de Ville, or by the winding, cobbled, pedestrian Rue Jeanne-d'Arc into the Rue Voltaire, the main street of the ancient town and once called the Rue Haute Saint-Maurice. The Rue Voltaire runs westwards from the Place de l'Hôtel de Ville, from which it passed through the town gate, the Porte de Verdun, long since destroyed. Joan of Arc arrived at this gate and entered Chinon on the 6th of March 1429, on her presumptuous mission to the Dauphin. The Rue Voltaire is as full of old houses as peas in a pod—and as tightly spaced. Houses of the fifteenth and sixteenth centuries are common, and some houses are as old as the twelfth century. There have of course been alterations, but the street remains an antique, as redolent of a distant time as a suit of armour. It would be even more interesting and symptomatic of its time if the authorities were to ban cars from it, for the car is a howling anachronism here, as well as a perilous nuisance—the street is anyway too narrow for motor-traffic.

A number of little streets and *ruelles* or alleys turn downhill from the Rue Voltaire. At a *carrefour* the Rue du Grenier-à-Sel descends. It was in the middle ages the Rue de la Juiverie, the centre of the Jewish quarter, until the Jews were persecuted and taken away for burning on the Île de Tours, the island on the point of which the bridge rests a pier or two. No. 30 in this street, a good fifteenth-century house, was once the Hôtel des Monnaies.

On the other side of the Rue Voltaire, a cul-de-sac leads to the painted cave which has some ancient murals. The cave is the entrance to an extensive system of underground galleries beneath the château, formed by the extraction of stone for building. Rabelais knew the painted cave and drank here 'mainctz verres de vin bon et frais'—many glasses of good fresh wine. It was the model for the Cave de la Dive Bouteille in *Gargantua*. The people of Chinon still store their wine in these temperate caves.

Look, as you go along the Rue Voltaire, for stone houses with corner turrets, for timber-framed houses with oversailing upper storeys, for an occasional renaissance window or other such detail. At the corner of the Rue Jeanne-d'Arc stands a timber-framed house recently thoroughly restored. Jutting from its wall at ground level is a low, square stone curb, the rim of a well. Joan of Arc is reputed to have set foot on this curb as she got down from her horse and to have stayed in the house while awaiting a summons to the château.

Farther along, the Grand Carroi, the great crossroads, was the centre of the old town, where a lane descending from the château crossed the Rue Voltaire and continued down towards the bridge. No. 44 in the Rue Voltaire is the Maison des États Généraux, dating from the twelfth to the fifteenth century, with a façade of the sixteenth; Richard Cœur de Lion is said to have died in this house on the 6th of April 1199. It has become a museum for the town of Chinon. No. 73 was the Palais de Baillage, in which Rabelais's father exercised his profession as a lawyer; it is now the Hôtel Gargantua.

The church of Saint-Maurice stands below the south side of the street. Originally built by Henry II of England on the site of a church of a hundred years earlier, it retains its romanesque nave and tower, with a spire of the fifteenth century. Joan of Arc came into this church to pray for her mission while she waited for the result of the deliberations of those appointed to determine her veracity. There is a statue of her, and she appears again in colourful modern glass in the south windows.

As you pass along the Rue Voltaire glance occasionally to the north. Between the houses here and there the château appears, high in the air, its white stone walls and towers sailing against the blue of the sky (plate 18).

There is much more to be seen in Chinon for the leisured visitor, much more of open or obscure detail to be sought out by patience and persistence. There is additional interest in the neighbourhood. Visitors with an interest in the arts may wish to go to Tavant, twelve kilometres to the east, for the sake of

26. Langeais, one of the last of the gothic fortresses

27. Wood-carving of the Holy Family on a house in Tours – it may be seen *in situ* in plate 20

28. Chenonceau. The original turretted renaissance château on the right, with the classical extension put up by Catherine de Médicis on Diane de Poitier's bridge

29. The recreated formal garden of Villandry

30. Azay-le-Rideau – the gothic–renaissance rhythm

the murals in the church there, while those with literary tastes will seek out the manor of La Devinière, about six kilometres to the south-west, where Rabelais, if he was not born there, certainly spent a part of his childhood. It is a simple little building of stone with a steep roof and an outside stone stair to the upper floor. If he was not born at La Devinière, then Rabelais was born in Chinon, where his father had a house that still stands on the corner of the Rue de la Lamproie and the Rue Jean-Jacques-Rousseau, the eastward continuation of the Rue Voltaire.

We leave Chinon by the main road, the N751, climbing in a steep curve round the château, and in a couple of kilometres turn off north on to the D16, a country road that brings us to the D7 beside the Indre, where the river winds and subdivides parallel with the more sedate Loire. We turn east and in three and half kilometres come to the château of Ussé, set on a hillside against the dark background of the northern margin of the Forêt de Chinon, and overlording the tiny village of Rigny-Ussé. The bridge over an arm of the Indre is perhaps the best place for a first, overall view of this château, which is said to be the original of the castle of the Sleeping Beauty in Perrault's fairy-tale; or you may go farther back to the raised embankment of the Loire—only a short distance, for hereabouts the two rivers flow so closely parallel that the Indre gives the impression of being a reluctant bride, anxious to escape union with the main river.

There has been a château at Ussé since the middle ages. It was bought in the second half of the fifteenth century by Jean Buell (who died in 1477), and was rebuilt by him and by his son Antoine, who in 1481 married one of the illegitimate daughters of Charles VII and Agnès Sorel. Antoine sold the château in 1485 to Jacques d'Espinay. After the Espinay family came a series of owners, ending in the Blacas family, who still own it.

The château was originally built as a complete square, with

an enclosed, well defended courtyard. In the eighteenth century the north side of this courtyard was demolished, opening the remaining three wings to a view of the valley threaded by the Indre and the Loire, and allowing the light and air freer entry. So what one sees now in the frontal view from the rivers is an open courtyard flanked by splendid towers with *poivrière* roofs. Look at these towers and think of Langeais, and through Langeais of Plessis-Bourré, which we have yet to see. Jean Bourré's hand and his style are seen again at Ussé in machicolations both decorative and practical, in the covered *chemin de ronde*, in the set-back tops of the towers above it, in the slope of the *poivrière* roofs, and in the barred chimneys that grow out of them. The old gothic spirit, the military spirit, has come to perfection in its old age. But though Ussé is a castle indeed, it is more humane than the sullen fortress that Langeais is, gayer in design and attractive where Langeais is repellent. Perhaps it is largely due to the beautiful white stone. Perhaps we of the twentieth century see in it, besides beauty and efficiency, a sense of high romance that was not perceived at all by the fifteenth century.

Visitors enter the park and climb a steep path to a space in front of a chapel, where one awaits a guide. What a beautiful chapel this is! Built between 1520 and 1538 it catches the elaboration of flamboyant gothic and marries it to the effervescence of the Renaissance. The west doorway, with a large shell hood, and over that a traceried window, beneath niches topped by thickly encrusted pinnacles, is a joy that deserves long and passionate looking. Inside there are dark, carved stalls with misericords against white walls of the finest masonry. Set in the wall is a beautiful and delicate piscina and credence, ornately carved in low relief, and purely, entirely renaissance. A doorway matches it. Here and there the initials C and L stand for Charles d'Espinay and his wife Lucrèce. An Aubusson tapestry relates the story of Joan of Arc, and there is a Virgin in faience by della Robbia.

The rising footpath rises to the château, and we enter a

courtyard of an uncomplicated elegance that extends in style from the gothic crocketed pinnacles of the dormers of the west wing to the Renaissance of the east wing (plate 25) and the more positive Italianism of the pedimented windows of the south wing.

More of the rooms of the château of Ussé are shown to the visitor than is the case with some other privately owned châteaux. The rooms have appropriate antique furniture, with a number of paintings and some excellent tapestries. One suite of rooms was furnished for the reception of Louis xiv. The bedroom, with its reeded pillars rising to corinthian capitals, takes the château of Ussé into the classical age. The bed, a four-poster hung with crimson damask under a shallow saucer dome, stands against a wall covered with the same material, and the pattern and colour are picked up again in the backs and seats of disk-backed chairs.

The *Belle au Bois dormant*, the Sleeping Beauty, may sleep still at Ussé, the château on its flowered terrace on the border of the hardwood forest of Chinon, beneath the high cones of the *poivrière* roofs. We leave her to her slumbers to seek out the château of Azay-le-Rideau, following along the D17 for fourteen kilometres beside the sub-dividing Indre. At the village of Quinçay road and Indre turn away from the Loire, and shortly thereafter we pass above the château d'Islette, which stands down by the river. Built about the same time as Azay and Chambord, it is evidently in style a plainer relative of its famous neighbour. Azay itself is three kilometres farther upstream, on the other side of the river and of the N75.

Azay-le-Rideau takes its name from one Rideau or Ridel who was seigneur of Azay in the twelfth century—the inhabitants of the little town of three thousand people call themselves 'Ridellois'. They live partly on a wood-working industry, partly on fruit-growing—especially apples and pears (you will see the orchards in the countryside), and partly on the making of a white wine that is good enough to merit the accolade of an *appellation contrôlée*—'Coteaux de Touraine'.

Ridel's château was destroyed in 1418 by Charles VII, who, angered by an insult from the Burgundians, who then held the place, stormed it and put the garrison and the inhabitants of the town to the sword, beginning with the captain of the guard. Charles burned down the château and for a hundred years thereafter Azay was known as Azay-le-Brulé, Azay the Burnt.

Early in the sixteenth century the ruined château was acquired by Gilles Berthelot, treasurer-general to François I. Berthelot, too busy to attend to the matter himself, gave his wife Philippe encouragement and the necessary finance to rebuild the château. Under the guidance of the master mason Etienne Rousseau, Philippe erected a fine jewel of a house rising directly from a moat fed by the Indre, and reflected in it to double the pleasure it gives to the eye. There are inevitable comparisons with the Chenonceau of Philippe's cousin Catherine Briçonnet, because of this setting in still water, and because of the feminine sensitivity and taste that is reflected in the elevations and in the plan of the rooms of the building. Architecturally the resemblances and the derivations are to be found rather in the François I wing at Blois.

In the 1520s a scandal broke out concerning the royal treasury. It was asserted that ministers had been helping themselves to the king's finances. One of these ministers, Jacques Semblençay, was hanged, perhaps wrongfully, as historians assert. Gilles Berthelot took the hint at once and fled abroad, never returning to France. The king, François I, in the belief that the château of Azay had been paid for out of his money, confiscated it. That is the reason for the presence on the walls of François's twisting salamander and the inscription 'Nutrisco et estingo'—'I nourish and I extinguish'. The ermine of his wife Claude de France is also here, with the more cryptic inscription 'Un seul désir', as though all she had ever wanted was the château of Azay and its feminine charm. After several subsequent private owners, Azay returned to the state in 1905 and its rooms now contain a museum of late medieval and early renaissance furniture, pictures, and tapestries.

The entrance to the château is serene and beautiful. A frontis-piece of two bays, flanked by pillars, rises through two storeys to a large and ornate dormer. The walls either side are relieved by string-courses, double and single, as at Blois, but at Azay there is a regularity and symmetry in the spacing of the windows and the intervening panels that is several years in advance of François I's wing at Blois. This spacing and the deliberate rhythm of the fenestration is seen clearly on the elevations rising from the moat. The round corner towers, the handsome machicolations, the pinnacled dormers derive from the middle ages and from gothic, but the rhythm of the fenestration, the symmetry, looks forwards towards the classical (plate 31). In some other things too Azay is more modern—for example in the staircase of straight flights under a ceiling ornamented with low-relief portrait medallions. Whether it is seen in sunshine that accents with its shadows the mouldings of the white walls, or floating on the mists that rise from the moat in the evening, or in the buttery yellow light of *son et lumière*, Azay is a château that stays in the mind as one of the jewels of the Loire valley.

The little town is proud of its château, proud of its 'camping' beside the Indre, proud of its romanesque church.

Our next aim is the small château of Saché, where Balzac stayed and wrote. We can go there directly by the picturesque minor road north of the Indre, by the D17 south of the river, or by neither of these, for we can make a detour by the D57 to Villaines-les-Roches. The attraction of this place is its basket-making, much of which is carried on as a home industry in the houses of people who live in caves. You may see all kinds of wickerwork things, including furniture, in the making, and buy whatever takes your fancy.

For a pleasant little château without pretensions, for a fetching *gentilhommière*, certainly go to Saché; if you are an admirer of Balzac, then you must go to Saché, for between 1829 and 1837 the great man came here frequently for months at a time as a guest of his friend M. Margonne, filling the house with his presence. Working all hours of the day and the night, stomping up and down and shouting out or growling the dialogue of his characters as he created them, Balzac must have been a trying guest; but M. Margonne endured him. At a little desk that seems absurdly feeble for the work that came into being upon it, Balzac wrote the whole of or parts of *Père Goriot* and much of *Le Lys dans la Vallée*—the valley of this latter book is that of the Indre between Saché and Pont-de-Ruan, a distance of no more than three kilometres, which Balzac describes in detail as the locale of his book.

The house is now a Balzac museum, with a collection of figurines of the characters of his *Comédie Humaine*, of caricatures of Balzac and of his friends, of the furniture he used and the bed he slept in, and of proofs of his books so thickly and so minutely corrected that the compositors in the printing-house refused to work on them for more than two hours at a time because the labour of putting the corrections into effect brought on eye-strain and headaches. A modern comp would be asking for 'Balzac money'.

The house has been too much altered to be of architectural interest, but it is pleasant enough and is one that any author would be glad to work in, looking for relief from its windows on to a garden of lawns and old trees (plate 25).

The last of the châteaux on our return journey to Tours is Villandry. The simplest way to reach this, though not the most direct, is to go back to Azay-le-Rideau and take the D57 past l'Islette, join the D7 at Lignières-de-Touraine, and turn towards Tours. A short distance outside Lignières you will see across fields full of fruit trees the old farm-house of Fontenay. It is built like a tiny château, complete with pepperpot tower, and stands safely within a surrounding defensive wall.

Beside the route all the way to Villandry caves open into the low cliff or bank that borders the south side of the road. The entrances are closed by gates, which are generally locked, but through these gates you may see boxes and casks, and perhaps growing mushrooms.

The road runs parallel with the river Cher. You may park under young pollard trees alongside the carriageway, opposite the château of Villandry.

The medieval château that stood here was called Colombiers; the name was changed to Villandry when the owner, Balthazar le Breton, became a marquis in 1619. His ancestor Jean le Breton had rebuilt the château in 1532 in an unexceptional renaissance style, retaining for the usual purpose of seigneury the old keep of Colombiers. In the nineteenth century the château fell on evil days and became badly neglected. It was bought by Doctor Carvallo in 1906 and restored. Carvallo determined also to restore the garden to a full renaissance style and sought information and authority for the designs. What we see today is the result of this work. The gardens are on three levels. You come to them through the château, where you are first shown the museum, which has a surprising Hispano-Moorish ceiling, and emerge on to a terrace (here your guide will inform you that he or she is not paid by the château but depends for a living on your tips). The view from the terrace reveals in one sweeping glance the plan of the garden. The upper stage is the water garden, with a large lake, and then comes the ornamental garden immediately below your perch, and beyond it the vegetable garden. The last two may not be immediately distinct, for both are designed on a highly geometrical plan, with small beds surrounded by diminutive hedges of miniature box (plate 29). The first reaction is a gasp of amazement, but for me, at least, the subsequent reaction is the realisation of the amount of labour expended in the construction and necessary for the maintenance of a garden that, despite the initial astonishment, must for those using it regularly quickly become a bore. Geometry may please a geometer, but there is too little variety here for most people, especially for anyone brought up on the English style of garden. The regimented little yew trees do not provide real relief. The old keep of Colombiers regards the pattern with a defensive solemnity. In the background are the roofs of the village, and rising from them is the short, stout spire of the eleventh-century romanesque church.

The D7 continues beside the Cher, passing at Savonnières a stalactite cave with petrifying springs, which you may enter. In this area there are many small caves used for commercial purposes.

The only thing of moment on the way to Tours is the view across the valley of the Cher and the Loire of the thirteenth-century château of Luynes, with which we began this chapter.

PART THREE

Anjou

*Candes to Angers
and the valley of the Loir*

Anjou

As is the case with Touraine, the name of Anjou does not designate any political or territorial division, and has not done so since the French Revolution. The territory that bore the name of Anjou is now part of the *département* of Maine-et-Loire. Yet the name of Anjou persists in common use and the people who live in this part of France call themselves Angevins. The reasons are not difficult to see. The name of Maine-et-Loire is too factual, too ordinary, too bare of connotation; it means nothing more than that the district is based on these rivers. While *Anjou*—there is a name trailing connotations like a robe of many colours shot through with the glories of a long history.

That history is full of bluster and battles and of attempts by one neighbour or another—of Normandy or Brittany or the Count of Nantes, or the Count of Touraine—to annex parts of Anjou to their own possessions. So the story is one of many defensive actions, of lands won and lost and won again, until in the person of Foulques Nerra the Count of Anjou took aggression to his neighbours. The relations of one count to another, of one family to its neighbours, are complex and involved, with many marriages undertaken for dynastic reasons or in the hope of ensuring peace. From the story there emerges Geoffroy the Handsome, who became known as the 'Plantagenet' from his custom of wearing a sprig of broom in his hat. He married Matilda, daughter of Henry I of England, and their son Henry became, on the death of King Stephen, Henry II of England, King of England and Count of Anjou, and through his wife,

Eleanor of Aquitaine, master of lands reaching down to the Pyrénées and half-way across France. Henry was one of the most powerful men in Europe.

But the Plantagenets were not a cohesive or disciplined family. They fought among themselves and squandered their resources. Their worst king, John, faced one of France's most able monarchs, Philippe-Auguste, who in 1203 wrested Anjou from John and so made it part of the kingdom of France.

Because of that distant connection it is sometimes said that the typical Angevin resembles the typical Englishman or shares some of his characteristics; but what kind of Englishman that may be you must judge for yourself.

After the time of Philippe-Auguste the countship of Anjou was bestowed by the king on members of the royal family. In 1246 Louis IX gave it to his son Charles of Provence, who became King of Naples and of Sicily. This was the origin of those empty titles claimed three hundred years later by René of Anjou, last of the counts. From Charles, Anjou passed to the Valois, and when Philippe of Valois became Philippe VI of France it was once more attached to the crown. In 1350 Jean-le-Bon gave the countship to his second son Louis and ten years later Jean raised it to a duchy. Louis's son Louis II of Anjou spent most of his time in his kingdom of Naples and the government of the duchy was carried on by his wife Yolande of Aragon, who on the death of her husband in 1417 became regent for her son Louis III. When Louis died childless in 1434 the duchy passed to René together with the title of King of Sicily and Naples. René was also Count of Provence and titular King of Jerusalem.

It could not be said that all of these counts and dukes spent their lives in Anjou. René was unusual in making his home in the duchy in the château of Angers, or in one or other of the smaller *gentilhommières* he built throughout his territory. With his deep interest in poetry, literature, painting, and music he made his court of Anjou one of the brightest and most civilised in France. He was popularly known as Good King René. His image comes down to us as that of an amiable and talented monarch, a gentle father figure. But when his son John died suddenly in 1470 René decided to leave Anjou to go to Provence, where he died in 1480. He left a will disposing of his duchy, but it was pointless. Louis xi of France had desired Anjou for years, and he now seized it.

Anjou is partly cattle-raising country with broad fields on the uplands above the rivers that water it, all tributaries of the Loire. To the north the rivers are the Oudon, the Mayenne, the Sarthe, and the Loir, uniting to form the Maine, which flows through Angers. To the south there are the Layon, a small river that joins the Loire downstream of the Maine, and the Thouet and the Dive, which join together south of Saumur. A mile or two on either side of the principal rivers fruit and vegetables are grown. The Saumurois specialises in growing mushrooms in the large caves in the *tuffeau*, and the cuisine of Anjou includes a variety of methods of dealing with these fungi. All of these products will be of interest to the tourist who is something of a gastronome.

The more obvious interest, however, is the growing of grapes for wine. The vineyards are found in a variety of places along the rivers. The best-known of the wines of Anjou is certainly the rosé d'Anjou, made from the Groslot, Cabernet, Gamay, and Cot grapes.

Although it has the largest of the châteaux of the Loire valley (in terms of area enclosed), the château of Angers—and at Saumur what was one of the most fascinating gothic creations—Anjou is often ignored by commentators on the châteaux of the Loire. This is not because of lack of interest, but rather because Anjou lies farthest from Paris and is therefore less accessible than is the Orléanais or Touraine. Certainly in Anjou châteaux are not so thick on the ground as they are in Touraine and the Blésois, but what there are are of interest and cover a wide band of time and of architectural style. From the military might of

Angers we may pass by degrees through the ornament of Saumur in its heyday and the more civilised comfort of Plessis-Macé and Plessis-Bourré to renaissance Brissac and the eighteenth-century sophistication of Montgeoffroy.

If it is relatively poor in châteaux, Anjou is rich in ecclesiastical buildings. The abbey of Fontevraud inevitably heads the list, together with the cathedral of Angers, where the particular type of roof known as the Angevin vault first appeared. There are many small churches that are worth a pause, and some of them worth more than that, as for instance the church of Cunaud. A minor curiosity of Anjou is the church with a twisted spire. Whereas in some countries church spires exist that have been twisted by accident, by warping or settlement of the timbers inside, in Anjou twisted spires appear to have been deliberately designed. One of the best-known is at Vieil-Baugé, but there are others at Mouliherne, Distré, Fontaine-Guérin, etc.

8. Candes to Saumur

Candes is still in Touraine, just within the modern departmental boundary, beside the junction of the rivers Vienne and
Loire. It stands on a narrow strip of ground at the foot of a high
and steep hill. Here the road runs so compressed between houses
and village shops that lorries have trouble in getting through.
In the middle of the village a little square or *place*, with a rough
surface, steeply inclined, rises to the church of Saint-Martin,
built on the site where Saint Martin died in the fourth century
—the village is properly called Candes Saint-Martin. The
church is what one comes to Candes to see. Built in the twelfth
and thirteenth centuries, it was constructed with a love and a
skill and a holy zeal that created a masterpiece. It stands
curiously aloof in its quality and seems to question what it is
doing here, but it is the parish church and at times of mass it is
alive and vibrant with those words that have echoed in its
stones for so many centuries.

The fortifications evident on the exterior, the machicolations
and crenellations, belong to a time more than three hundred
years later, when the countryside was made perilous by maraud-
ing bands who took advantage of the confusion of the Hundred
Years War. When these rapacious fellows appeared the people
of the village would lock themselves with their priests in the
church and defend themselves as best they could.

The north porch is large and richly carved. The swooping
ribs of its high roof descend at the centre to gather in a sheaf on
the capital of a single slender shaft. The splays of the doorway

are enlivened with figures of fearsome monsters—what nightmares were there in the minds of the carvers that they thought
it necessary to frighten the worshipper before he entered the
church? Perhaps the monsters represented the torments of hell,
which might be avoided by respect for the apostles in the niches
above and by devotion to the Christ, whose figure, now mutilated, appears in the tympanum over the door, between the
Virgin and Saint John.

Inside the church it is the height of the narrow nave that
first impresses, a height enhanced by the slender columns in
clusters soaring to carved capitals under a roof whose Angevin
vaulting carries the eye still further upward.

Though Angevin vaulting occurs outside of Anjou—as in
fact it does at Candes—it nevertheless seems to have been the
invention of Angevin masons. Whereas in normal vaulting of
the twelfth or thirteenth century the central rib of a bay is
horizontal and straight, and the transverse ridge ribs are also
horizontal and straight, with the central keystone on the same
level as the points from which these ribs spring, in Angevin
vaulting the keystone is higher than those points and all ribs
curve upwards. The effect is as though every bay were domed
like a parasol. The stresses must have been more difficult to
calculate and the masonry had to be precise, but the Angevin
mason solved his problem with joy and perpetuated a style that
he must have first attempted with some trepidation.

The capitals, though high in the air, are worth some study.
Some of them retain a little colour, a reminder that churches
that are today plain and austere were in the middle ages
colourful or even gaudy. The two aisles, north and south, are
vaulted in the same Angevin manner as the nave. The chapel in
the south transept next to the choir is reputed to be on the site
of Saint Martin's cell, where he died in AD 395; a recumbent
statue commemorates him. One of the treasures preserved in the
sacristy is a phial of dried blood that Saint Martin collected
from the Theban legion, the legion that, under the command of
Saint Maurice, refused to sacrifice to idols and was massacred

by Diocletian; now dry and powdery, the blood is, I dare say, a sovereign and miraculous cure for some malady or other.

A roughly cobbled lane toils upwards past the west end of the church. Signposted 'panorama', it ascends through a hamlet or two, where you chase the route from corner to corner, and then becomes a country lane between hedges and fences. Finally, you trudge up on to a down-like hill crest and there before you is a most splendid view. Below your feet, beyond the slated roofs of the houses of the village, the Vienne and the Loire meet on a point of white sand, opposite a bright and sandy beach scattered with pioneering bushes. The beaches are bordered by woodlands that seem at first to extend to the horizon, where, in the far distance, shines the silver sphere of the nuclear power station near Avoine. Open fields appear to nestle among the woods. Long, sandy *îlots* in the river are crested with trees. The best time to see this view is in the spring, when the leaves have a tender green that hangs like a shimmering mist in the air; or in the autumn, when each tree assumes its own colouring of yellow or russet, and its own time to change, and the woods are variegated from the remnants of summer's green to the dying fire of the falling leaf.

Nothing more than the departmental boundary divides Candes Saint-Martin from Montsoreau. The main road runs alongside the Loire, and we take a step or two along it to find ourselves in Anjou, the province in which the English Plantagenet kings, the longest of all dynasties of English kings, had their origins: historians often prefer to call them the Angevin dynasty.

Montsoreau offers water-sports from its beautiful beach on the Loire, and it has a château built in the fifteenth century by a man called Chambes, whose family earned a doubtful reputation for the ferocity of its men and the seductiveness of its women. The military aspect of the family is reflected in the severity and fortification of the château. The façade seen from the road once rose directly from the river. Nowadays the château houses a museum of the Goums—Arab soldiers under French officers in Morocco; they were used in war as scouts.

The church of Montsoreau introduces us in advance to our next port of call, the abbey of Fontevraud. The little church of Montsoreau contains a suite of stalls that came from the abbey when it was pillaged during the Revolution, and also a seventeenth-century painting, a Crucifixion, in which, at the foot of the cross, an abbess kneels in adoration, her face simple and sweet, her crozier over her shoulder.

We follow the road inland, the N147, past the château of Montsoreau, and in four and a half kilometres enter the small town of Fontevraud or Fontevrault, where the sloping Place de la Mairie has on one side the gateway to the abbey and on the other the ancient parish church of Saint-Michel next to the Hôtel de Ville.

In its heyday the abbey of Fontevraud was among the most remarkable in France, and one of the largest. Founded by a hermit called Robert, from the village of Arbrissel in Brittany, in a clearing of the forest where there was a spring of fresh water, the Fons Ebraldi, it grew rapidly in Robert's lifetime from a simple hermitage, probably in the beginning of huts and caves, into a true monastery. When Robert died in 1117 he was buried in the church and was later given an elaborate monument. The tomb was destroyed at the Revolution, when the marble was sawn up and used to build chimneys in a neighbouring château, which still exists.

The foundation, which became mixed, of men and women—but mainly of women—attracted royal and noble patronage. The counts of Anjou, who became kings of England, favoured it and chose it for their burial place—the abbey church still contains the recumbent figures of two English kings who were also counts of Anjou, and of two English queens. Throughout seven centuries the abbey flourished and expanded and it was said eventually to contain five thousand persons—an exaggeration of a kind common to monasteries and convents in any country. Nevertheless, it was undoubtedly large and well peopled. Within the encircling wall there were no less than four distinct religious foundations. The principal one was that of Sainte-Marie, called the Grand Moûtier ('*moûtier*' is an old form of the word monastery), which was for nuns following the contemplative life. Saint-Benoît was a hospice for the sick. Saint-Lazare was, as its name implies, a lazar-house for lepers, to which, probably, anybody with a sore or a scrofulous skin was likely to be sent. La Madeleine is also self-descriptive; it was for repentant 'daughters of joy'. Finally, there was a fifth foundation, Saint-Jean-de-l'Habit, a monastery for men, which was, very properly, outside the wall. Men were necessary in this female organisation to act as almoners, as priests to administer the sacraments, and as clerks and notaries to manage the possessions and dependencies of the abbey. For the abbey came to have fifty dependencies scattered throughout Europe.

All these foundations, including that of Saint-Jean, were governed by an abbess, who was called the 'head and general of the order'. Between 1115 and the extinction of the order at the Revolution thirty-six abbesses held this position. It was one of power and prestige, and princesses of the royal blood, sisters and daughters of kings, did not refuse the veil and the appointment. Fifteen of the abbesses were of royal blood, five of them Bourbons. The last of these Bourbons was the daughter of Henri IV. One of the most notable of the abbesses was Marie-Madeleine-Gabrielle de Rochechouart de Mortemart, who was a sister of Madame de Montespan. Louis XV sent four of his daughters to be educated at Fontevraud, and so that he might with propriety, such was protocol, sit down when he visited them, he created the abbess a duchess.

The Revolution turned out all the nuns and monks and devastated the abbey—and incidentally destroyed the livelihood of the town that had grown up at the abbey gates to provide food, materials, and services for the inhabitants. The many beautiful possessions the revolutionaries found were some of them destroyed, some of them sold, all of them scattered. Of the hundreds of books and precious manuscripts in the library none remain here; occasionally a book with the abbey's arms on the binding turns up in a sale room. Various paintings, sculptures, pieces of furniture, and other things found their way into churches up and down the country, as for example the stalls and the painting at Montsoreau. Thirty pieces, including a splendid seventeenth-century altar, were acquired by the village church of Saint-Michel of Fontevraud.

Napoleon in 1804 turned the empty monastery into a prison, spending two million gold francs on the conversion of the buildings to this base use. A prison it remained until 1963, when the buildings were transferred to the department of historic monuments. The bolts and bars have gone now and a large part of the complex still in existence, but not the whole of it, is open to the public.

The public, however, are not allowed to wander about at will. Guides with the usual bunches of keys usher you around, leaving too little time for the contemplation for which the Grand Moûtier was built. They lock the doors as you move from part to part, although nearly every room is empty—perhaps they fear that visitors will seek immortality by writing their names on the walls. At our visit an American woman, anxious to record every interesting detail with her camera for the folks back home, was constantly being left behind and locked away from the rest of the party.

The part of the foundation you will see belongs mostly to the Grand Moûtier. Its curious kitchen, called the Tour d'Évraud, is the first thing to catch your eye as you pass from the forecourt into what was the secluded part of the convent (plate 31). The base plan of the kitchen is eight apses on an octagon (five only remain); each apse has a conical roof and a chimney under a small conical cap. The plan then changes to square for a short space of roof from which sprouts another collection of cone-topped chimneys. The plan now changes back to octagonal, for the large, central octagonal cone, which is topped by another chimney. All the roofs are covered with stone in an eye-catching pine-cone pattern. The total effect is strange and esoteric, but it is based on the presence inside of a series of hearths, each of which was engaged in cooking for the nuns. I know of no other kitchen that is quite like this one at Fontevraud. There was something similar at Saumur, according to the illustration of that château in the Duc de Berry's *Très Riches Heures*, but it has long ago disappeared. Another, very simple, still exists at Montreuil-Bellay. Fontevraud's kitchen dates from the twelfth century.

The abbey church of the Grand Moûtier also dates from the twelfth century, an impressive building, grandly romanesque. Notice as you enter the lavish and involved carving of the capitals and the arch of the doorway. The interior is bare stone, still and austere, and stone too are the three domes by which the nave is roofed—could such domes be the origin of the later Angevin style of roofing? The domes and the intervening arches rest on clustered piers, the capitals of which may be by the same hands as the carving of the doorway.

In the south transept lie the four figures of the English royal house of Anjou. The two kings, Henry II and Richard Cœur de Lion, rest with their crowns on their heads and their hands holding sceptres that are placed straight along the middle line of the body. Eleanor of Aquitaine, Henry's wife, has a book open in one long-fingered, ascetic hand, as though she had been interrupted in reading it; it was Eleanor who brought to Henry the vast domains that extended his possessions to the Pyrénées. Isabelle of Angoulême, the second wife of King John and Henry's daughter-in-law, has her hands crossed on her breast, above a narrow belt that gathers her loose gown about her waist. The bones of these four persons rest in the crypt. The English royal family have several times asked for the return of these remains so that they might be interred at Windsor or in Westminster Abbey, but this has never been agreed. The two kings and the two queens lie here in Fontevraud because during their life this was their country and this was their choice.

A door from the south transept leads into the cloister, three sides of which are round-arched and renaissance in style, the fourth side the original gothic. The cloister garth, with straight paths criss-crossing a green lawn enlivened by young pollard trees, is a pleasant place and it must have given relief to the secluded nuns who walked here to study their books or simply to relax from their gruelling devotions.

The chapter-house, the *salle capitulaire*, stands on the east side of the cloister, the common arrangement in religious houses. A large rectangular chamber, as Continental chapter-houses invariably are (it is in England that one finds octagonal and circular chapter-houses), it was the meeting-place of the body of nuns who, like a little parliament, discussed and advised and assisted the abbess in the government of the abbey. Because its function was important the chapter-house, especially inside, was always given architectural emphasis. Some very splendid chapter-houses exist, and here at Fontevraud is a good example. The several bays of round romanesque quadripartite vaults gather their strongly profiled ribs into sheafs to rest on central pillars with ornate capitals. The floor is chequered with black and white figured or lettered tiles, on which you may see the RB of René de Bourbon, the winged and crowned initial L of Louise de Bourbon, the blazon of the Bourbons with three fleurs-de-lys, the salamander of the Valois, and some other designs. The semicircular spaces where the vaults abut against the walls are filled with paintings of the life of the Virgin done in the fifteenth century by an Angevin painter called Thomas Pot, and there is also a series of portraits of prioresses and abbesses. In one of these portraits Marie-Madeleine-Gabrielle de Rochechouart de Mortemart kneels at a prie-dieu, while at her feet a child, Mademoiselle de Blois, daughter of Louis XIV and Madame de Montespan, dressed in heavy satin, sits and looks abstractedly towards the viewer. The abbey was not a school but occasionally royal children were confided for their education to the care of the abbess, and one cannot help thinking that these children must have endured a thin and humourless life.

The refectory, a vaulted gothic gallery much longer than it

is wide, as though it were an enlarged cloister, glows with light from two tiers of later windows. It is now quite empty, an echoing space that must in its day have been noisy with the sound of crockery and of cutlery or china, if not with conversation—enclosed monks and nuns commonly ate in silence, listening to a reader intoning a chapter of the Gospel or of some devotional work.

The parish church of Saint-Michel in the Place de la Mairie, outside the walls of the abbey, was built from the twelfth to the fifteenth century, and is of interest for that reason, but its principal attraction is the collection of pieces from the abbey. The magnificent gilt altar of the time of Louis XIII, too rich and too large for a small provincial church, must be imagined in its place inside the bare stone walls of the abbey church, bringing life and colour to a building that appears today, however beautiful as it undoubtedly is, as bare and still as a skeleton. Paintings, too, adorned the walls of the abbey church, and a number of them are to be seen here in Saint-Michel. They include a vivid, late sixteenth-century Crucifixion, with a crowd of people around the cross who are not the people Christ would have seen but are men and women, ladies and housewives, soldiers and civilians, of the time of the painter, Dumonstier.

We now go across country by minor D roads for about fifteen kilometres to find the hill town of Montreuil-Bellay beside the river Thouet, a tributary that enters the Loire downstream of Saumur. At Montreuil-Bellay the river flows in a picturesque setting at the foot of an old water-mill, behind which on a cliff rise the defensive walls of the château and the steep roof, with a flèche, of the church of Notre-Dame. To the right of this the high towers of the château proper seem to leap upwards from the trees along the river side.

Montreuil-Bellay was a walled town and more than half of its medieval town walls remain, with a principal gatehouse, the Porte Saint-Jean, to the south, on the road to Thouars. It has the latter part of its name from the du Bellay family, one of whom held the place for three years against his suzerain Geoffroy Plantagenet and gave in eventually, in 1150, only because of starvation. To make sure that such resistance should not happen again Geoffroy destroyed the fortifications. The château was rebuilt in the fifteenth century by Guillaume d'Harcourt. The plan, or lack of plan, within the château walls suggests that Guillaume chose to erect his buildings on the foundations of previous structures that had been laid down *ad hoc*.

The entrance is made across a moat and through a gatehouse or *châtelet* flanked by two huge cylindrical towers with very strange tops—basically a conical roof, which, however, is almost obscured by four tall dormers facing in four directions, each with a pointed gable. The present appearance does not suggest that these towers were of obvious utility for defence. There are no crenellations, no machicolations. In fact, it is noticeable about Montreuil-Bellay that these defensive works are absent. Crenellations were for archers, machicolations for dropping unpleasant things on people attacking the walls. Both were obsolete or obsolescent in the fifteenth century, when a gunner could stand off and pound the walls to bits with cannon-balls. The designer of Montreuil-Bellay possessed a more realistic and forward-looking mind than had, for example, Jean Bourré at Plessis-Bourré and Langeais. He built his towers, other than the châtelet towers (the tops of which may be later), with flat platform roofs strong enough for cannon to be mounted on them. Offence was his kind of defence.

In the courtyard, with the various buildings so curiously disposed, there is a sense of enclosure, of being shut away from the world, which the trees growing there perhaps serve to enhance. But go into these buildings and it soon becomes evident that, as in other châteaux of the fifteenth century, the comfort of the inhabitants was an important consideration. So much so that the château of Montreuil is still inhabited.

The medieval kitchen was modelled as a more simple version

31. The surprising
kitchen (Tour
d'Evraud)
and the
abbatial
buildings of
the abbey of
Fontevraud

32. Young lovers
– a tender
wood-carving
on the
Maison
d'Adam in
Angers

33. The *châtelet* or gatehouse of the château of Saumur

of the Tour d'Évraud at Fontevraud—not in its decoration but in its general plan. There is also a kind of sauna bath, a stone-walled, stone-floored room, with another room below in which a servant stoked a fire and occasionally threw water on the glowing coals to provide the steam—the bather could communicate with him through a pipe in the wall, to tell him to stoke up the fire, to throw on more water, or to stay his hand.

One of the things well worth seeing is the principal stairway, which rises very gently on steps alternately dark and light in colour, so gradually that a horse could go up them—and indeed the Duchess of Longueville did ride a horse up there.

There is a guide to show you round. He or she carries a portable tape-recorder, switching on the commentary as you enter each room. There are tapes in various languages, and you may choose which one you will listen to. The English version is spoken in very good English, but an occasional oddity of speech betrays that it is written and spoken by a Frenchman. A room filled with suits of armour and medieval furniture is described as containing 'middle-aged antiques'.

The church of Notre-Dame has an unusual façade, with a deep-set rose window, but the building appears to have been too much restored to be of great interest. Originally the chapel of the château, and ambitious in size for that purpose, it was consecrated in 1484.

We leave Montreuil-Bellay to cross the bridge, with its attractive view of the château above the river, and take the N138 northwards towards Saumur. Near to that town we pass through Distré, which has a small romanesque church the spire of which has a distinct twist—one of many such spires in the province of Anjou.

Amateurs of ecclesiastical ruins may prefer to leave Montreuil-Bellay by the N761, in order to visit the abbey of Asnières, while those who love roses may, if the time is mid-July, like to go to Doué-la-Fontaine, where people live and breathe and adore and cultivate roses. In July they present a grand floral spectacle in what are called the Arènes, which are not Roman but an ancient open-cast stone quarry.

The abbey of Asnières was founded at the beginning of the twelfth century in what was then a deep and secluded forest. The trees did not conceal it from marauders, however, and it was several times sacked and damaged. In the nineteenth century the ruin was used as a stone quarry, and today all that is left is the central tower of the church and not much more than parts of the walls of the nave. Not a great deal, but as every- where in France the veriest ruin rates a franc or two for admission. The remains are sufficient to show that Asnières was an abbey of fine quality.

Doué-la-Fontaine, which is preceded by a well preserved windmill, also has a ruin, if not of an abbey, then of a depen- dency of a priory. The church of Saint-Denis was an outlier of the priory of Cunaud and was collegiate, that is it was served by a body of canons, who sat in stalls in the choir during services. Partly romanesque, partly in the Angevin style, the building has notable capitals carved with fantastic animals. Rather more realistic animals may be seen in a zoo on the outskirts of the town.

The N160 leads directly to Saumur, joining before Bagneux the road coming up from Distré. Bagneux has a megalithic dolmen, the most important of about fifty of these things in the Saumurois; it is in reality a kind of covered stone passage, probably serving a funerary purpose. It stands in an enclosure and you inquire at the Café du Dolmen.

Saumur is a place of ancient habitation that has contrived to grow into a busy yet not very large town—though the numbers of cars parked along the quays and on the Cale alongside the river suggest an affluent city. It has developed for the greater part on the left bank of the Loire and on a long island in the river, with which it is connected by the many low arches of the Pont Cessart. Near the centre of the town a rocky knoll is crowned by the château, the dominant building.

Among many industries of Saumur that of wine is the most interesting to the visitor. The Saumur wine district extends down to Montreuil-Bellay. The grape is the Chenin blanc, which produces by the *champenoise* method a dry or semi-dry fizzy or sparkling wine. The wine is stored in extensive caves, some of which were dug out of the cliff fourteen hundred years ago as refuges against bandits.

In the sixteenth century, when Protestants in France were strong enough to demand secure centres in which they might live and practise their religion, Saumur was one of their most important places. It had a famous Protestant academy, founded by the governor, Duplessis-Mornay, appointed by the Protestant Henri of Navarre, who later was to become King of France as Henri IV. The revocation in 1685 of the Edict of Nantes, the edict that gave Protestants the right to practise their religion, destroyed Saumur's position as a place of Protestant security. So many of the Protestant residents then left the town that its prosperity was crippled. Only recently has the population returned towards the figure it had in the seventeenth century.

Groups of young men in smart, light-coloured military uniforms may be seen in the streets of Saumur. They are cadets of Saumur's famous school of cavalry, founded in 1768 to take young officers leaving the cadet school of Saint-Cyr. The cavalry school is now also a school of armoured warfare. The cadets in 1940 determined to hold up the Germans as long as possible, and many of them were killed or wounded in the attempt. In this action, and in the war in general, the buildings on the island and on the north bank were badly damaged, while the castle was hit by more than a hundred shells.

The cavalry school mounts a spectacle at the end of July in which both horses and tanks show their paces.

The Place du Bilange, a widening of the main street, the Rue d'Orléans, before it meets the river and the Pont Cessart, is a suitable central point from which to begin an exploration of Saumur. The crossing with the quays is very busy, with a

gendarme controlling the traffic. Cars in movement and cars
parked by the roadside import an atmosphere of constriction
and fervour all at once. More cars park on the lower quay,
called the Cale, and the view of the town and the château from
the bridge, which Michelin recommends, has more often than
not a foreground of multi-coloured shining metal, not only itself
visually unattractive but also destructive of what is attractive.
The quay and the Cale were once part of the Loire, which
flowed at the foot of a hoary tower that you might suppose to
be one of the oldest buildings in Saumur, such is its appearance
of medieval strength and defence. This is the Hôtel de Ville.
In fact the oldest part of it is sixteenth century. It is worth a
moment's digression to wander into the courtyard, where the
different periods of the building are more obvious.

At week-ends a market is held where the quay narrows.
Markets anywhere have an interest of their own and in France
they are generally lively, varied, and voluble. Clothing of all
kinds, some of it second-hand, shoes, sweets, watches, jewellery,
handbags, are neighbours on the temporary stalls that are put
up for a few hours on the quay below the towers of the château.
There is something as medieval about a market as there is about
those towers.

The Rue de la Tonelle leads away from the quay to the Place
Saint-Pierre and the church of Saint-Pierre, which hides
behind an early sixteenth-century front a nave and choir partly
romanesque and partly, in the upper half, of the purest
Angevin style of gothic. The tall arches appear taller under
these rising parasol-like Angevin vaults. The church contains
two sets of early sixteenth-century tapestries, one of the life of
Saint Peter, the other of the life of Saint Florent. Several
incidents may appear on one tapestry, as on one of the Saint
Florent series, in which the saint is shown being beseeched by a
mother for help for her son lost for three days in the river; the
next illustration shows Florent presiding while fishermen draw
the boy alive from the water. In a third incident Florent, with
an angel at his back, suppresses a winged dragon that had been

annoying the people of what the legend calls the town of Meur—presumably Saumur.

One of the oldest parts of the church is the south doorway, which is romanesque and of the twelfth century. It is a noble work of five orders and richly carved.

The Grande Rue, rising southwards from the Place Saint-Pierre, is, despite its name, a narrow little street. It serves to bring us into the Avenue du Dr. Péton, and we turn left in this to find the château—or to arrive at it if 'to find' is otiose for a building that has been plainly apparent from most parts of the town. Why it is apparent the climb up the Grande Rue will have explained. The château of Saumur, as many châteaux do, stands on a steep mount, the vantage point of the district. The mount, of course, attracted fortification from an early period. The present building dates from the fourteenth century, and is the work of Louis I, Duke of Anjou, and of his successor, also Louis. As it is shown in the *Très Riches Heures du Duc de Berry*, an illuminated manuscript interrupted by the death of that duke in 1416, we have a terminal date for its completion. The château that appears in that book is marvellous, a fairy castle full of imagination and wonder, yet set upon solid stone for necessary defence—on high windowless walls with a glacis to deflect shot. Above this, out of reach of scaling ladders, the windows begin. The four strong vertically ribbed, polygonal corner towers rise to pepperpot roofs bordered by crenellations and crowded fantastically with fanciful chimneys, spires, and pinnacles. Every pinnacle bears a large gilded fleur-de-lys (Louis I of Anjou was the king's brother), and above every fleur-de-lys spun a gilded weather-vane. None of this decoration has survived. The illustration in the manuscript is in every other detail accurate and exact, as may be seen by comparison with the castle as it is today, but all the fancy has gone and the present impression of the château of Saumur is of a strong, medieval military castle that disdains fancy.

Between the years 1454 and 1472 René of Anjou made a number of alterations to the château, especially inside. The exterior was still splendid. René remarked how it glittered in the sun—'il rendait grand lueur quand le soleil luisait sus'. René was a poet with a poet's eye for detail and effect. When all that fine top-hamper disappeared is uncertain, but if it was still there when René died in 1480 and the duchy of Anjou passed to the Crown of France, it was probably no longer to be seen when Henri III of France granted Saumur as a stronghold to the Protestants. Duplessis-Mornay lived in the château and garrisoned it with a company of soldiers, and he employed an Italian engineer called Bartolomeo to build the surrounding outer wall—a wall designed specifically against cannon and built eighty years before Vauban made his name with his adoption of similar angular plans.

The end of the toleration of the Protestant religion in France was also the end of the château's great days. It was thereafter neglected and used for base purposes, as a barracks or a prison, until in 1908 it was bought by the town and turned into a museum. In the past few years this museum has been reorganised and modernised and it is today full of beautiful things beautifully displayed. It is in fact two museums, the museum of decorative arts on the first floor and the museum of the horse on the second floor—the latter a collection of spurs, saddles, bits, stirrups, and of bones of the prehistoric ancestors of the horse.

The museum of the decorative arts is of such high quality that I would like to counsel you to spend a whole day wandering about among its varied and magnificent exhibits. But my advice is rather not to go in at all, unless you are of a tougher fibre than I am. For the authorities insist that you go in on a guided tour as a member of a party, and if this system is objectionable elsewhere, it is positively insane in a public museum. It is not compulsory in other museums, not even in the Louvre. At Saumur you have no choice. You will be confined with the guide to one or two rooms at a time, and though you may stray from the guided party there will always be that crowd of people obstructing some of the exhibits in turn. The guide can discuss, of course, only the principal items before he is ready to unlock the door into the next room or section; as far as he and his party are concerned, more than half of the exhibits might as well not be there.

The car park for the château is in what was a moat up against the wall built by the Italian Bartolomeo. Above the wall rise the polygonal pointed roofs of the principal towers. You climb the wall by a stairway and come to a large courtyard in which a flight of shallow steps leads up to a pretty *châtelet* or gatehouse, with a machicolated bartizan above the entrance, flanked on each side by a tourelle with a shining pepperpot roof—the single, faint survival of the roof-line the château once possessed (plate 33). The inner courtyard of the château still has something of the prison appearance, which must have been more intense when all four wings were intact; but the western wing was demolished in the eighteenth century and now its site is a platform with a view of the town and the river and of the multiple arches of the bridge. In the foreground the church of Saint-Pierre sends a slender spire into the air from the pyramid roof of its central tower, and a little farther off along the river the spire of Saint-Nicolas answers.

In the centre of the courtyard a circular wall looks like a well, but it is in fact an air-shaft to an underground chamber that was used to store rainwater. The well proper, complete with its massive wooden winding gear, is in a small modern building near by; the gear was also used to raise provisions, brought to the foot of the well-shaft along a tunnel.

The masons of Saumur were experts at their trade and spared no pains, or were not allowed to spare pains, to produce excellently built walls, pierced by rectangular windows with traceried heads. Beside the well-house, situated in what must have been the extreme corner when the west wing still stood, is the principal stair tower, for the greater part embedded in its wing. It was an awkward situation for what was the main accent of the courtyard, minimising the ornament of its large canopied niche and its four ornate balconies, which, in the fashion of Azay and Blois, are open to the air.

You may climb from the courtyard (without a guide!) up another stairway to the roof of the watchtower or walk on the battlements for wide views of the valley of the Loire and the tributary Thouet. To the east you will see the huge dark, shining dome, topped by a cupola, of the church of Notre-Dame-des-Ardilliers, to which is attached the convent of the Oratoire in a late renaissance building. The church was in part built by Richelieu, in part by one of the king's ministers Abel Servien, in part by the contributions of the king. It contains a huge altar-piece by an Angevin sculptor called Biardeau and, in the Richelieu chapel, a statue of the Virgin that is described as having not the slightest artistic value, but which is none the less venerated. The dome was damaged during the war and afterwards was rebuilt.

To the south of the château lies the church of Notre-Dame-de-Nantilly, which is worth a visit for its tapestries. These include the 'Siege of Jerusalem by Titus', the 'Angel Musicians', and the 'Life of the Virgin'. They are interesting for their studies of the costume of the period, especially one in which the Virgin is shown being tucked up in a very twentieth-century-looking double bed, while a midwife (Saint-Anne?) hands the newly born infant to a servant girl. The legend on a ribbon says 'Cy est la nativité noustre dame'. There is no hint of the stable at Bethlehem. Two of Nantilly's tapestries are in the château museum; one of these is the only thing I remember at all well of my journey through that museum. It shows a conceit, a fancy-dress ball of the fourteenth century, the 'dance of the savages', in which the guests came in costumes covered with fur or feathers—fascinating and in some way epicene.

9. Saumur to Angers

We leave Saumur by the N751 on a road that runs for many kilometres beside the Loire, a beautiful road with the many-islanded river on one hand and on the other a succession of small riverside villages that are ancient and possess centuries-old churches to prove their antiquity. They have old houses too, but as these are village houses of no particular architectural merit, following with little change a pattern that was set who knows how long ago, it is difficult to say how old they really are. But they have charm, do these crumbling walls under jumbled roofs.

We come first to the twin villages of Saint-Hilaire-Saint-Florent. At Saint-Hilaire you may see the sparkling wine of Saumur in course of manufacture by the *champenoise* method, the method by which champagne is made. There are cheaper and more productive ways of making a bubbly wine, but the result is less good.

Saint-Florent has an abbey that is sometimes called Saint-Florent-le-Jeune because there is another Saint-Florent, le-Vieil, a long way down the Loire, beyond Angers, and that too has an abbey. The abbey of Saint-Florent, founded in the seventh century, was bothered by thieves and warring barons and the monks moved their foundation from one place to another, hoping for peace and security. The advent of the Normans drove them from Saint-Florent-le-Vieil into Poitou. The monks returned eventually to Anjou, only to have their monastery burned down by Foulques Nerra. At last they came to their present site, and built an abbey there in the eleventh century. The crypt of that old abbey remains, but the greater part of the claustral buildings were rebuilt in the eighteenth century in a pleasant classical style. Today they house the order of the Bon-Pasteur, an order of nuns, who will allow you to see the remains of the old abbey.

Along the road to Chênehutte-les-Tuffeaux there are caves dug deep into the hillside and fitted with gates. Some of these are used as workshops by the local artisans, some as storehouses, and some, very extensive, are used for growing mushrooms, utilising for this purpose the horse manure conveniently provided by the school of cavalry at Saumur. One of the caves is open as a mushroom museum. At Mimerolle, which has a particularly lovely stretch of the Loire, Balzac stayed at the house of a friend and finished writing *Le Lys dans la Vallée*.

Les Tuffeaux has a sturdy and ancient church by the roadside, a church that once, before the riverside road was built, rose directly from the water; or so Michelin says, a statement that is somewhat at odds with the presence of a good romanesque doorway facing the river. The square tower, with its romanesque openings of the eleventh century, and its Chinese-hatted apse below, is a picturesque object which, except for the pyramid roof, looks its age.

Two kilometres beyond Chênehutte-les-Tuffeaux we come to Trèves, with practically nothing of a village, but with a squat little romanesque church and by its side a huge fifteenth-century round keep glowering unprotectively down at the church. For connoisseurs of the picturesque this is indeed a find, and it would be a find for photographers if it were not that you would need a stand camera with an extreme wide-angle lens and a rising front to do any kind of justice to it. The tower was the *donjon* of a château built by Robert le Maçon, chancellor of France in the early days of the royal predilection for the Loire valley, that predilection that rubbed off on to the ministers and servants of the Crown. He died in 1443. The strong stone walls of that formidable château have disappeared with the wind, leaving only the *donjon*. It is still private property, however, and you are not allowed into it.

The church, with a funny little polygonal stone steeple, very short, has a fine air of antiquity. The present tower and steeple are a replacement for an earlier and broader tower that probably fell. That tower had six round-headed openings on each side, and some of these openings may still be seen partly obscured by the roofs of the transepts and the sanctuary. The church contains a large porphyry font of the twelfth century with grimacing masks, and an intricate carved reliquary of the fifteenth century. A recumbent figure, damaged, represents Robert le Maçon.

Less than a kilometre brings us to the next village of Cunaud or Cunault. It may be remarked that each of these small villages alongside the Loire is placed at the junction of a road coming down from the plateau to the south, which gave them some minor importance. A band of monks fleeing from the Normans settled momentarily at Cunaud, where they had been granted property, and then continued to Tournus in Burgundy, where they founded a Benedictine monastery. Later a group of them returned to Cunaud to found a priory here, and in the twelfth century they began to build a church. Not for them the modesty of such a church as Trèves—which was also a priory church. At Cunaud the ambition was higher, the aesthetic achievement more profound, and evidently the finances more adequate. In this lonely place on the bank of the Loire, which here, in effect, is a double stream because of a long central island, the monks erected a church so lovely and so impressive that it is commonly called an abbey church—which it never was. Yet it is not really large—it simply gives the impression of being so. The building went on for years, as is the way with churches, and the style changed as time progressed. The thirteenth century arrived with the pointed arch, and the pointed arch is evident at the west end of Cunaud; but the rounded arch of the earlier period is the one that contributes most to the general impression. The nave was lengthened by three bays in the thirteenth century, and these three bays have Angevin vaulting.

Facing the west end stands the prior's house, built in the sixteenth century and altered in the nineteenth; the changes to the façade are partly hidden by climbing plants. The house is renaissance in style, with mullioned and transomed dormer windows surmounted by ornate gables that, in their ornament, betray the coming conversion to the classical.

The prior's house looks across a dusty little *place* to the west façade of the church. During the troubles of the Hundred Years' War this front was lightly embattled, but the crenellations are not very serious efforts at defence. Hundreds of English churches have battlements erected as ornament that would be as useful in defence as these at Cunaud are. The monks were evidently of no mind to spoil their beautiful façade by additions too castle-like. Two blind pointed arches flank a large round-headed doorway of several plain orders. Its principal ornament is a statue of the Virgin in the tympanum, a statue in the round and now severely damaged. It was a fine piece of work that seems to hold within itself the gentleness of motherhood; it has suffered the malevolence of savagery, besides the erosion of time. The face is battered, the two hands of the Virgin are amputated, and the head of the Child seated on her lap is gone too.

Pass beneath this figure into the church. You at once descend steps to the level of the nave floor, and so for a moment your occupation with these will delay the exclamation of wonder this interior may evoke from you. The nave appears long and softly lighted and its dignity and proportions are gently emphatic. It is mostly plain stone today, but once the walls and the capitals were painted in colour. Some fragments of murals remain, including a large Saint Christopher, carrying on his shoulder a Child with a basin-cut hair style. Christopher walks in water with his feet among fishes of kinds that might be found in the Loire. The capitals of the columns throughout the church deserve admiration. There are over two hundred of them, all carved with little figures engaged in various pursuits. Objects of interest in the church include a Pietà, deeply adored, and perhaps too much restored—it was originally of the fifteenth century; a large and sophisticated figure of Saint John, once part of a sixteenth-century Calvary; a fifteenth-century Saint Catherine in wood; and a thirteenth-century house-shaped shrine in wood alternatively said to be walnut or oak. The shrine is carved with figures of apostles, of angels, and of the Virgin, and was made to take the relics of a local saint, Maxenceul. Gilt and coloured at the time it was made, it is an impressive piece, all the more interesting because shrines of wood of this period are not common.

Gennes, two kilometres downstream from Cunaud, is a larger place, with a bridge over the Loire to the opposite village of Les Rosiers. The church of Saint-Eusèbe rises on the hillside of Gennes, in a position that gives a view of the Loire extending for a long distance upstream and downstream. The nave of the church is a ruin, but the twelfth-century tower still stands, with a spire twice rebuilt since the Hitler war. A monument to the cadets of the Saumur cavalry school commemorates those who died in that suicidal attempt to hold up the Germans along the river.

The tower of Gennes is a noble piece with an interesting series of carved stone brackets of great variety—ornamental patterns, curling snakes, grotesque masks, and a little man peering cheerfully between his own raised legs.

We continue beside the Loire from Gennes by the D132 and in four and a half kilometres pass through le Thoureil, an attractive village that was once a river port from which the apples grown in this district were shipped—the church tower contained a light to guide the boats. Apples are still grown in the area and in the spring you may come upon signs inviting you to follow a 'blossom route' through the orchards. The church has romanesque foundations and inside you may see two wooden shrines reminiscent of that at Cunaud, but three hundred years later, renaissance in style, and far more sophis-

ticated in design and conception. These two shrines belonged to
the abbey of Saint-Maur, which stands two and a half kilometres downstream. Today a classical building of the seventeenth century stands in place of the abbey founded by Saint
Maur, a disciple of Saint Benedict, in the sixth century. Some
remains of the older buildings are to be seen, notably a gable
wall bearing a beautiful strapwork cross of the Carolingian
period. In the thirteenth-century chapel on a hill, built by
Saint Martin on the site of the oratory of Saint Maur, parts of
the sarcophagus that contained Saint Maur's body have been
discovered.

Less than two kilometres distant there was yet another
religious house beside the Loire, the priory of Saint-Rémy-la-
Varenne, a dependency of the Benedictine abbey of Saint
Aubin at Angers. What remains is a building partly occupied
as a presbytery. The lower walls are gothic, the upper parts
renaissance with charming dormers, and something remarkable
—round recesses from which busts project, as though people
inside were leaning out through the openings. The church
near by dates from the tenth century.

A country road, the D55, crossing the N761, brings us in
thirteen kilometres to the town and the château of Brissac.

Brissac is a hill town descending towards the Aubance, a
tributary of the Loire. It descends also towards the château
standing in a park surrounded by cast-iron railings. The site
does not today appear an obvious one for a fortress, but the
château erected here in 1434 by Pierre de Brézé was certainly
a fortress, a fortress of an impressive kind. Two huge corner
towers remain from this château, handsome in their strength.
Circular, with closely spaced machicolations and covered wall-
walks below set-back upper parts, the style seems to be that
of Jean Bourré. But this was before Jean Bourré's time and it
seems evident that the inspiration for the towers of Plessis-
Bourré and of Langeais had at least some of its origins in
Brissac.

In 1502 René de Cossé bought the seigneury of Brissac and

founded here a family that included four marshals of France—
a remarkable record. Two of his sons became marshals, and his
grandson another. The fourth was Charles de Cossé, seventh
Duke of Brissac. Charles decided to rebuild the medieval
château, which had suffered damage during the wars of religion. His architect was Jacques Corbineau. The new château
was to be in a rich renaissance style, four tall storeys high, with
an asymmetric frontispiece tower one storey and a dormer
higher. It made a huge façade and promised a large and expensive building. The architect began by pulling down the medieval château between the two fortified corner towers and started
to build his new château between these two towers. That the
towers were meant to come down as well is apparent from the
rough junction of the masonry where the renaissance work
abuts against the medieval walls. But in 1620 money or energy
or both were exhausted and the work stopped.

The result is bizarre. In no other château does the middle
ages shoulder up against the high Renaissance as it does at
Brissac. Certainly it is picturesque, and just as certainly it is a
shock to the eye. As someone has said, it is a new château half-
built in an old one half-demolished.

The new château was to be of the very best quality. The
masonry is superb, the design skilful and inspired. The frontis-
piece, with its five storeys, is as though five Roman temple
façades were stood one upon the other, rising from a terrace
that enhances the impression of great height. And all this is in
the white *tuffeau* limestone of the district, whose fine grain lends
itself excellently to carving and bas-relief.

The rest of the château, behind the façade and the medieval
towers, is more sober, more classical in appearance, even dis-
appointing after the liveliness of that impressive introduction
of two periods.

The Cossé family has lived in the château continually since
the sixteenth century. As houses with such long periods of a
single habitation often do, Brissac has conserved much of its
contents of various periods, and you walk through a house that

is still alive, with its own furniture, paintings, and tapestries. The principal rooms have the thickly beamed ceilings of the seventeenth century, with the ornamental painting of the beams unaltered.

In the cellars under the château several antique objects of the wine-making business are displayed, and there is a bar where you may taste the wines of the district.

Marie de Médicis and her son Louis XIII met in the château following the encounter known as the 'drôlerie des Ponts-de-Cé'. Marie, for a time regent during the minority of her son, had gained a taste for power and could not easily brook her son's taking the reins into his own hands. She several times rebelled or intrigued against him and the unsuccessful encounter of her forces with those of the king at the Ponts-de-Cé was a minor incident for which, none the less, a commoner or a noble would have lost his head. Louis warily forgave his mother.

The Ponts-de-Cé, eight kilometres distant on the road to Angers, is a village with an interminable street continued by a series of bridges over arms of the sub-dividing Loire and over the Authion canal. It was the scene of many sanguinary encounters. One commander seeking to cross the Loire and believing that the eight hundred harlots who accompanied his soldiers would be in the way in any action, had them all thrown into the river. Here too took place the encounter of the forces of Marie de Médicis and Louis XIII mentioned in the previous paragraph, the 'drôlerie des Ponts-de-Cé'. Louis, probably believing that the men who fought on his mother's side did so unwillingly, pardoned them all and granted them the full honours of war.

A château on the island of Saint-Aubin, built in the twelfth century, defended the passage of the river. Only parts of this remain, including a broad fifteenth-century polygonal tower.

The importance of the bridges at Ponts-de-Cé was that any invading army that succeeded in crossing them was only eight kilometres from Angers.

34. The *donjon* of Plessis-Bourré

35. Plessis-Macé: the restored balcony in the courtyard

36. A cave-house at Troo

10. Angers

Angers is the largest of the towns or cities in the length of the Loire valley we are exploring. Its river, however, is not the Loire, but that shortest of rivers, the Maine, which just above Angers unites the waters of the Mayenne, the Sarthe, and the Loir, and continues through Angers to extinguish itself, after a total course of fourteen or fifteen kilometres, in the Loire. Its affluence turns the Loire into a river that is navigable down to the sea.

Angers has been a provincial capital for longer than history can reach into the past. It was the principal centre of the Gallic people called the Andecaves, whose name is preserved in the modern name of the town and of the province.

The château beside the river dates from at least the ninth century. This was one of the châteaux from which Foulques Nerra, Count of Anjou, sallied forth upon his brutal and ambitious expeditions against his neighbours, and from which, in his sudden crises of contrition, he undertook his pilgrimages in expiation of his aggression, The château was rebuilt about 1140 by Geoffroy Plantagenet and some time after the year 1230 was rebuilt again in a larger form by Saint Louis, who surrounded the town with walls strengthened by thirty towers. His intention was that the town should be a stronghold against the English and their allies the dukes of Brittany. Saint Louis's walls remained until 1812, when they were demolished and replaced by boulevards built along their site, as was done in Paris—a city or town *enceinte* comprised not only the wall itself but also a bank and a moat, and the whole gave ample space for a wide street. The boulevards show the former line of the walls clearly both on the ground and on the map. The enclosure on the east side of the Maine is approximately rectangular, with the château in the south-west corner; that on the west side is roughly triangular. The protective function of the walls was continued across the river by suspended chains. Bridges now cross where these chains hung; these bridges are still known as the Pont de la Haute Chaine and the Pont de la Basse Chaine.

In the ninth and the tenth centuries Angers was the centre, the capital, of the *comté* of Anjou. A second line of counts of Anjou, of the blood royal, held court in the château in the thirteenth and fourteenth centuries. Jean-le-Bon, King of France, in the fourteenth century made Anjou a duchy in favour of his son Louis, who may be remembered in our estimation as the duke who ordered the making of the tapestry of the Apocalypse, which now, after the passage of five hundred years, once more decorates his château of Angers. The last duke of this line was René, the poet, musician, and patron of arts and letters.

The oldest part of the town is on the east bank, where the château and the cathedral stand. The extension to the west, beyond the river, rose largely as a working-class quarter around the convent, founded by Foulques Nerra in one of his moments of benevolence, of Notre-Dame-de-la-Charité, soon to be known as the abbey of Ronceray from a venerated statue of the Virgin discovered among brambles (*ronces*). A second focus of development of this quarter was the twelfth-century hospital of Saint-Jean. The quarter beyond the Maine, *outre la Maine*, became known, as it still is known, as the Doutre, and whether you lived *ça Doutre* or *là Doutre*, this side or that side of the Maine, was regarded as socially distinctive.

In the late middle ages and during the Renaissance Angers became a prosperous place and its prosperity was reflected in its domestic architecture, in the houses of bishops, nobles, and merchants, from at least the fifteenth century onwards. Many interesting houses survive in the streets, as you may discover for yourself by walking about observantly. Some of the better ones are now museums or art galleries. Less important houses were built on timber frames, many of them with diagonal timbers nogged with brick after the fashion we have already encountered in Tours. The streets of the older quarters exhibit a variety of timbered façades. These houses have interesting carvings on the corner posts or on the uprights. You will find them, for example, in the Rue Saint-Aignan and the Rue des Poêlliers in the old town and in the *Doutre* in and around the Place de la Laiterie. The finest of the timber-framed houses, however, is the one most conveniently found, the Maison d'Adam in the Place Saint-Croix next to the east end of the cathedral.

The château is an obvious place to begin an exploration of the town of Angers, both because it is a land-mark plainly apparent to any visitor and because you may park your car in the Place du Château, beneath the banded black and white towers of the formidable castle, or in the continuation the Promenade du Bout du Monde—which may not in fact be the end of the world but does come to an elevated dead end with views of the busy quays and the river, and over to the Doutre.

The plan of the château is an irregular pentagon, four sides of which are reinforced by round towers—seventeen of them altogether. The fifth side, towards the river, has none of these towers—it is a survival from the previous château of Geoffroy Plantagenet and was probably retained unaltered because the river, lapping its foot, was considered adequate defence. The walls and the towers are of a black schist or slaty stone. It is a dull material and the château would have a dismal aspect if it were not for the contrast of the bands of white calcareous stone that appear like hoops around the towers. The seventeen white-banded towers give distinction to the château, but the character remains that of a strong military fortress that was intended to announce its strength to any adversary. The strength and character must have appeared even more obvious when the towers were their original height, several feet above the tops of the walls, with roofs *en poivrière*. The upper parts were taken down in the sixteenth century, during the religious wars, when the governor Donadieu Puycharic was ordered to demolish the château for fear that it might fall into the hands of the Protestants—although Angers was Catholic the neighbouring town of Saumur was a Protestant stronghold. Puycharic was reluctant to demolish the château and he proceeded slowly and unenthusiastically. He had got no further than taking off the tops of the towers when times changed—the Protestant Henri of Navarre became king as Henri iv.

The château is entered from the Promenade du Bout du Monde by a bridge on the site of a drawbridge over a deep moat. The moat is dry and in the grassy bottom, in as it were a deep gorge, a herd of deer browse and play. It seems a curious place to keep them.

The first impression you will receive on entering the court-yard is of the vastness of the area the château walls enclose. A great deal of it is empty space or garden. Of what might have been here in the time of Saint Louis you will have no inkling, not even of the strong keep that must have existed. Each period has adapted the château to its own particular needs, demolishing, building, and demolishing again. Once a palace of dukes, the château degenerated into a prison, then an asylum, and finally a barracks. It was not until after the Hitler war that it was transferred to the department of fine arts for preservation as a building of historical value.

So you may not find the interior of the courtyard of the château of Angers quite what you expect. As you come through the gate you are faced by the chapel built by King René's mother Yolande of Aragon in the fifteenth century. Attached to the chapel on the right-hand side are the king's quarters. To the left is a formal sunken garden bordered by rows of trees. Overlooking the garden is the governor's lodging, built by René and subsequently altered. That seems to be all that there is. However, behind the chapel you will find a twin-turreted gothic *châtelet*, the gatehouse to what was the ducal or royal quarter, and next to it a long, flat-roofed modern building, only just lower than the château walls, erected especially to house the tapestry of the Apocalypse made for Louis 1, Duke of Anjou, in the fourteenth century and possibly displayed for the first time, when it was new, in this very château of Angers in a building long since vanished.

The art of the *tapissier* and the quality of the tapestries that survive in the town or in the province are the pride of Angers and of Anjou in general. There are many tapestries scattered throughout Anjou, but this tapestry of the Apocalypse, of high artistic achievement and inestimable monetary value, is the jewel of them all. It was made to illustrate a vehement but recondite and enigmatical religious story, the concept of sin and damnation in relation to the second advent formulated by a mind that believed in the presence or the coming of a vengeful god.

Commissioned by Louis for one cannot tell what particular purpose the tapestry of the Apocalypse was a vast work comprising a number of related pieces (seventy-seven pieces survive), and it is difficult to imagine what building it was intended for. It must have measured when it was complete more than three hundred and thirty-five feet long and sixteen feet in height, and few indeed could have been the châteaux with a hall providing so much free wall space on which to hang it. It was made in the last quarter of the fourteenth century, at a time when tapestries were popular for both ecclesiastical and domestic use. Entries in the register of the treasury of the dukes of Anjou record payments for parts of the tapestry as they were completed—as on the 7th of April 1377 a payment of one thousand francs for the weaver 'sur la façon de deux draps de tapisserie à l'histoire de l'Apocalice qu'il a faiz'. The weaver was Nicolas Bataille, who worked to sketches prepared by the painter Hennequin de Bruges. Hennequin derived his inspiration from the illuminated manuscripts of his day. The Apocalypse of Saint John, emphatic, obscure, and full of strange and powerful images, was then a popular subject and there were many manuscripts to which he could refer, enriched by the careful and colourful miniatures that delighted the wealthy patrons of the art of the book. A number of these books survive, precious relics in the libraries of states and of great institutions.

The detective work carried out, or that may yet remain to be carried out, in tracing the influences and origins of the tapestry of the Apocalypse, would make a fascinating story. There are interesting clues to be discovered, as for example in the inventory of the library of Charles v in the Louvre, made in 1373, where it is recorded that a volume of the Apocalypse had been lent to the king's brother, 'Monsieur d'Anjou, pour faire son beau tapis'. The book is now manuscript No. 403 in the Bibliothèque nationale in Paris. The loan proved a long one, for the book was not returned to the king's library until 1492—but that date has nothing to do with the completion of the tapestries; it is simply an extreme example of the notorious reluctance or neglect to return borrowed books.

Hennequin divided the story into seven sections or 'chapters'. Seven, of course, has always been a magic number. Each chapter began with a tall scene the full height of the tapestry showing a bearded old man under an ornate architectural canopy. He reads a book or a phylactery and appears to have no interest in anything else. There follow two rows of seven scenes each, on backgrounds of blue or red, in many instances variegated by simple arabesque patterns. There were originally strips above and below these groups representing the sky and the earth, and there were others bearing legends explaining the illustrations in the fourteen scenes; but these have not survived. Because of the disappearance of the wording—not to speak of the obscurity of the original book—it is in many instances uncertain what is meant by the illustrations or who all the persons in them may be. It is, for example, not known who the large introductory figures under the canopies are meant to be—unless, I suggest, they may represent the presiding deity, God himself. It seems unlikely that they represent Saint John, for John appears as an onlooker in most of the scenes, expressing horror, amazement, fear, etc. Some things, of course, are clear enough. There are the terrible horsemen who have so inflamed the gothic imagination from the time of the tapestry designer to the Hollywood of the twentieth century, there are the serpents and the fierce lions (curiously, horses in the tapestry also have faces very like those of lions), there is the woman clothed with the sun and with the moon at her feet (who is represented as the Virgin), and above all there is the seven-headed beast, which appears over and over again in different guises.

The minatory story of the Apocalypse loses nothing of its frightfulness in the faded blues and reds of the Angers tapestry and in the calm of the airy gallery in which it now hangs. You may contemplate it at your leisure and, praise be, without a guide; if you wish to have a guide you may hire an individual 'teleguide' receiver, a thing like a tape-player, to which you listen as you walk around; it is not heard by other people. There are also on the walls opposite the tapestry various explanatory photographs, some of which show the relation of the pictures to manuscript illustrations. The whole display of the tapestry is extremely well done.

The tapestry has endured a chequered history and it is wonderful that so much of the series has survived. When they were fresh and new the pieces would have been carried round from château to château in the wake of the movements of the duke—tapestries were so much portable wallpaper to be hung up wherever the owner for the time chose to make his home. Perhaps the tapestry of the Apocalypse was too large to suffer many of these transfers. However, in 1400 it was carried to Arles to serve as part of the décor for the wedding of Louis II of Anjou to the rich and beautiful Yolande of Aragon, a marriage of which one of the fruits was to be René, last duke of Anjou and titular king of Sicily and of Jerusalem—the most amiable ruler in the long story of the Loire valley. It is interesting to note that the background of one of the pieces of the tapestry of the Apocalypse is decorated with the recurrent letter Y. The Y may not be for Yolande, but if it is not—and the tapestry as a whole seems to have been complete before the year 1400—it is not known what it stands for.

The tapestry pieces were rolled up and stored from time to time, as in 1476 at the château of Baugé. In 1480 René bequeathed the tapestry to the cathedral of Angers. There for three centuries it was stored away, to be brought out in part once a year and displayed in the cathedral or in the neighbouring palace of the bishop. The annual exhibitions ceased in 1767, interest in and respect for things gothic having then fallen to nothing, and in 1782 the chapter tried, without success, to sell the tapestry. It had become, in effect, so much rubbish, and the pieces came to be used as horse-cloths, as covers to keep the frost off orange trees, and as wads to be stuffed into cracks in walls to keep out the wind. In 1843 what remained was put on sale again, together with other odds and ends. The lot was bought by Bishop Angebault, who saw the aesthetic and historical value of the work. He bequeathed the tapestry once more to the cathedral, where it was again displayed on feast days.

Further series of tapestries may be seen in the château of Angers. The tapestry of the Passion, woven in Flanders in the late fifteenth century, retelling the story of the Crucifixion, is displayed in the chapel built by Yolande of Aragon—up against the windows and not well seen. The chapel is a high and broad chamber of stone with a good vault; near the altar is a room or recess elaborately fronted in which Yolande and her son René would sit to hear mass.

The remaining tapestries at the château are various. They include the fifteenth-century 'Lady at an organ', in which an elegantly gowned lady plays a small organ apparently in the open air, against a background of *mille fleurs*. This is one of the most attractive tapestries I know of, to be remembered with that of the Lady of the Unicorn in the Musée Cluny in Paris.

The amateur of tapestries should follow the Maine upstream to cross by the Pont de Verdun or the Pont de la Haute Chaîne to the old Hôpital Saint-Jean. The tapestries to be seen here are in piquant contrast with those of the Apocalypse, by which none the less they are said to have been inspired. These tapestries at Saint-Jean, ten in number, are large, modern, brightly coloured on a dark ground, and form a series called the Chant du Monde. Woven at Aubusson, they were designed by Jean Lurçat, who saw the tapestry of the Apocalypse in 1938 and received from it a desire to create for the twentieth century a reply to what Hennequin de Bruges had created for the fourteenth. The gestation was long. It was not until 1957 that Lurçat began work on the tapestries now on display at Saint-Jean in the vast ward of the medieval hospital. The theme is the mind of man today, his hopes and his disappointments, his fears and his nightmares set against his faith—the best and the worst of man. The style is modern and abstract and the meaning complex, so that these tapestries require for their understanding as much attention as does the Apocalypse. That they are a major work of the art of tapestry design and manufacture in any period there can be no doubt.

The setting for these works is the twelfth-century aisled *salle des malades* of the ancient hospital, a building in the finest Angevin gothic style, with Angevin vaulting to all three aisles. The patients in the hospital—and this chamber would have been packed full with two or three in a bed—looked up to those parasol roofs, outlined by delicate ribs, which curve down like the branches of trees to rest on two rows of slender columns. It is surprising how well twelfth-century gothic and the twentieth-century tapestry accord.

At one end of the hall the pots, shelves, and cupboards of a seventeenth-century pharmacy survive. At the other you may penetrate behind Jean Lurçat's 'L'Eau et le Feu' to find the cloisters of the old hospital.

The Hôpital Saint-Jean, in the Doutre, is a little apart from the old town, and if your time is restricted, or you mean to leave Saint-Jean until later, then I suggest you leave the Place du

Château to climb the Rue Toussaint. On the right of this street the ruins of the abbey of Toussaint, with a large wheel window, stand in a colourful garden. Behind it, facing the Jardin des Beaux Arts, stands the Logis Barrault, built in the fifteenth century as a private house and now the museum of fine art; it has a collection of the extraordinary life-like busts carved by the sculptor David d'Angers. The house is a fine example of the domestic style of the Renaissance, and it may be compared with the Hôtel de Pincé farther north. A corridor inside has one of those ribbed vaults in which successive keystones are set alternately to left and right; we saw something similar at Chenonceau. The design must have complicated the mason's work frightfully, and the resulting untidy effect is more novel than beautiful.

West of the Logis Barrault rises an enormous twelfth-century tower with the truncated remains of a steeple. This tower, the Tour Saint-Aubin, was the detached belfry of the church of the abbey of Saint-Aubin. It looks across the Rue des Lices and along a broad but short side street, the Mail de la Préfecture. The interest of this street is that it was the nave of the abbey church and you may imagine the young trees that now line it as the columns of its aisles. The abbey and its church appear to have disappeared entirely except for that great detached belfry, but walk down the Mail and look through the windows of what is now the préfecture. You will see—and it is astonishing, whatever your expectation—the richly carved, round arcades of a romanesque cloister and of a chapter-house doorway. This survival surprised the workmen who came upon it in 1836 hidden behind false walling and plaster probably put up in the seventeenth century, when the abbey was rebuilt—the préfecture is part of that rebuilding. A great many changes take place during centuries of use, and the préfecture is now a building of many periods. Most of it is superficially uninteresting, but little perception is required to notice that some of the rooms, notably the reception hall, have ancient detail. It may be no more than the curve of a roof or the presence of a column.

Another romanesque doorway, which led to the refectory, was discovered in 1852. Who knows what else may be hidden in this préfecture?

The abbey of Saint-Aubin was founded about the year 535 by the Gaulish king Childeric. It became Benedictine and was rebuilt in the twelfth century in an ambitious style; it is to this period that the discoveries in the préfecture belong. The two doorways that remain are not small or insignificant and certainly were not easily hidden several hundred years later when the abbey was rebuilt a second time. Projecting bits of carving that would have protruded through the plaster of the new walls were ruthlessly chopped off. Not a qualm disturbed the workmen or those who directed them. They thought little of what they were shutting away from sight. What the twelfth century had carved with piety and delight, what the twentieth century finds so full of quaint charm and of high aesthetic interest, an intervening generation believed to be worthless.

The capitals of the doors and arcades are carved with broad, strongly veined leaves and intertwined stems, and with human and animal figures. On the refectory doorway warriors dressed like Norman soldiers, with tall pear-shaped shields, fight evil dragons. Below this, winged angels adore the Lamb of God and wave censers. Next, two ferocious lions, more accurately observed than those of the tapestry of the Apocalypse, tear a boar to pieces. The chapter-house doorway is plainer. The most interesting work is contained in the spandrels above the twinned arches of the cloister arcade. In one, David, with a large hammer-like object in one hand, swings his sling in the other as he faces the giant Goliath, who, already falling, holds his spear upright and is helmeted and dressed in mail like a Norman knight. To the right of this scene David cuts off the giant's head and on the left he presents the head to Saul. Another arcade has a high-relief figure of the Virgin in majesty, flanked by two censing angels. Below this, marvel of marvels, pictures carefully painted in colour on flat stone in the thirteenth century have survived as they probably would not have survived if they had not been covered over for so long. In the centre a towered and fortified city or castle represents Jerusalem. On either side of this the story of the massacre of the infants is graphically told.

It is marvellous, too, in France, that you may go in and see these things free of charge.

An even older building lies hidden away among the streets to the north of the préfecture. The collegiate church of Saint-Martin stands on the site of a Roman street and a second- to third-century Christian cemetery. The crossing and the choir of the ancient church remain. The handsome arches of the crossing, of white stone banded with triple rows of tiles, date from the ninth or the tenth century and have a suggestion of the oriental about them—the Moors penetrated deep into France and were turned back only a few miles south of the Loire valley. The sturdy, plain arches of Saint-Martin's echo the similarly banded arcades of Cordova and other Moorish buildings.

The Rue Saint Aubin, narrow for most of the way, leads into the Place Saint-Croix, from which the east end of the cathedral of Saint-Maurice rises like a polygonal cliff pierced high up by two-light windows of plate tracery. The *place* is of moderate dimensions and but for the cathedral and one other building is commonplace. The other building is the Maison d'Adam, a sixteenth-century timber-framed house with the timbers in the diagonal fashion popular in its day in various towns of the Loire valley. Its polygonal corner tower and its three tall and steep gables add a note of the picturesque and of piquant contrast, which is enhanced by the plain plastered seventeenth- or eighteenth-century walls of its neighbours. One may imagine that in the sixteenth century all the houses of a prosperous area resembled the Maison d'Adam and the pattern of the diagonal timbers and the lozenge shapes they form would have been dazzling in so enclosed a space as the Place Saint-Croix. But look more closely. The builders of timbered houses such as this sought individuality in the carving on the uprights of charming or amusing little figures. The Maison d'Adam has its name from one of these groups, of Adam and Eve, now vanished. There are, however, several other figures on this house, and among them my favourite is a sentimental little carving of a pair of seated lovers, an Adam and Eve of a later day (plate 32). His left hand is about her shoulder, his right holds her left hand, his sword hangs loose beside him, and he has apparently just said something to her that has disturbed her modesty.

The Maison d'Adam looks across a side street, the Rue Montault, to a building with plain romanesque windows and two round towers with pepperpot roofs. This is the former palace of the bishops, and here for a time were kept the tapestries of the Apocalypse. The building, dating from the twelfth century, is one of the oldest in civil use in France.

The west front of the cathedral is reached through the Place Freppel. The west front overlooks a brief *place* that turns into a long straight street, which descends in an even slope to the river. But this street, the Montée Saint-Maurice, is no ordinary street, but rather a kind of processional approach to the cathedral, designed to enhance the west front. Partly paved with stone sets, it has up the centre a series of flights of stairs that lead directly to the west door. The cathedral, its lower part at first obscured, seems to rise out of the ground as you climb.

The outline of the west front is tall and narrow, with two dissimilar and not equally tall spires. Between these two spires, and eased in as it were with a shoehorn, stands a sort of elongated classical temple, which was added in the sixteenth century by Jean de l'Espine. It is very out of keeping, an extreme example of the difficulty of cohabitation of the Renaissance or the classical with gothic.

The west doorway is large and ornate and is dominated by Christ seated in majesty in the tympanum, surrounded by the symbols of the Four Gospels—the angel of Saint Matthew, the lion of Saint Mark, the eagle of Saint John, and the winged bull of Saint Luke. Below this is a strange plain lintel with an arch the shape of a walrus moustache. This curiosity was inserted by the canons of the cathedral in the eighteenth century, when, wishing to facilitate the exit and entry of processions, they removed the central post from the doorway. On each side of the entrance four tall figures solemnly regard the visitor: Moses, David, and the Queen of Sheba may be recognised.

The cathedral is cruciform, without aisles. It stands on the site of a previous church built about 1140 and burned down within a few years. The architect of the building erected in its place—the present building—retained the outer walls of the destroyed church. This gave him a nave over fifty feet wide, which he determined to vault in three large square bays. The width was exceptional for the period and in order to obtain greater strength in the vaults he domed them. The time was the mid twelfth century and this was perhaps the first appearance of Angevin vaulting, which was to become popular throughout the west of France.

Contrary to the usual practice of beginning a church at the east end, the rebuilding of the cathedral of Saint-Maurice was begun at the west. The progress of experience and of knowledge in the building of Angevin vaults may be seen as one goes from the west door towards the choir. The nave vaults are on single ribs like broad, square girders, forming a simple cross from corner to corner. They look perhaps as though the builder, rather uncertain of himself, was playing it by feel, groping towards something not done before. Now look at the vaults of the crossing and the transepts, completed eighty years later. The ribs are more numerous, more delicate and elegant, and they appear to have been designed confidently, with knowledge of the weights and stresses involved. The choir, vaulted about the same time, is similar. The depth—or height—of the vault is not obvious from the ground. It measures about ten feet vertically up to the keystone of the vault above the apex of the crossing arches dividing the bays.

How the Angevin vault developed further may be seen farther north in the choir of the church of Saint-Serge, and of course in the Hôpital Saint-Jean in the Doutre.

The furnishings of the cathedral need not detain us for long.

There is a series of tapestries, mostly from Aubusson, but they hang too high and are too dimly lighted to be seen satisfactorily. Where these hang now the tapestries of the Apocalypse were hung on certain feast days; the gain in the quality of viewing in their new building in the château is too obvious for comment. The stained-glass windows are more easily seen and should be studied, for the series, ranging from the twelfth century to modern times, is a practical manual of the history and development of stained glass from its early days. Three twelfth-century windows on the north side of the nave, rich in blues and reds, show the passion of Saint Catherine of Alexandria, the death and the funeral of the Virgin, and the martyrdom of Saint Vincent of Spain. The choir has sixteen windows of the thirteenth century, with the illustrations typically set in circular medallions one above the other in the long narrow openings of the period, which here are in pairs. The great thirteenth-century rose windows of the transepts are filled with fifteenth-century glass by a known designer, André Robin. The south windows of the nave are modern.

Wander about in Angers, choosing the little streets where you can, narrow little *ruelles* walled on either side by the cliff-like frontages of seventeenth- and eighteenth-century houses. An occasional older façade, perhaps of a timbered house, attracts attention, or suddenly a more elegant stone front to a renaissance mansion appears at a turn or a bend. Such houses were built at a time when the contiguity of other houses was not something that a noble or rich merchant disdained, at least in a town. Such is the Maison de l'Estaignier in the Rue Saint-Aignan, with its polygonal entrance tower, the door and windows of which have no regard for symmetry. Or you may come upon the Hôtel de Pincé, north of the Place du Rallie-ment, the busy hub of the city. The Hôtel de Pincé was built about 1535 to the design of Jean de l'Espine (who designed the 'temple' between the cathedral towers) for J. de Pincé, mayor of Angers. The Hôtel de Pincé has the inconsequential and unreasonable charm of the high Renaissance, the opulence of ornament in fine stone and the outrageous disdain of all reasonable balance. The embedded stair tower has the doorway squashed up in a corner. Attached to the side of this tower is a round turret topped by a dome on which rests a large and curious architectural finial. Pilasters and niches hang on the walls, and above are ornate dormers sprouting pinnacles. Inside, the main staircase is roofed with a fan vault upheld by ribs spreading from a central pillar like the branches of a palm tree. There are beautiful fireplaces, contemporary with the house. In the nineteenth century the house was the home of the Angevin painter Bodinier, who bequeathed it to the town. It is now a museum or art gallery containing the catholic collection of another painter, Turpin de Crissé—it includes Greek and Etruscan vases and European and Oriental prints, enamels, etc. There is also a collection of prints of the history of costume.

11. Around Angers

A number of short journeys may be made from Angers, to see places of interest in the surrounding countryside. It is a countryside largely given over to fruit and vegetable growing and to the rearing of cattle. Except along the main roads—to Nantes, to Poitiers, etc., and in the neighbourhood of Angers at going-home time for the factories and offices—there is peace and quiet in plenty and space in which to wander at will.

Serrant, our farthest point west, lies about eighteen kilometres from Angers beside the N23 towards Nantes. The château here, constructed over a period of a hundred and fifty years from 1545 to the early eighteenth century, is a medley of the renaissance style merging into the classical. The earliest part, designed by Philibert de l'Orme, was of a single storey. In the seventeenth century the house was raised by a storey and corner towers were added. In 1636 the château was bought by its third owner, Guillaume Bautru, whose granddaughter married the Marquis de Vaubrun. The marquis, lieutenant-general of the king's army, was killed at the battle of Altenheim. The marquise continued the building of the house until 1705 and in memory of her husband erected the chapel to the design of J. Hardouin-Mansart, and placed inside it a monument by Coysevox. Later the house belonged to the Irish family of Walsh, one of whom was created a count for his work in support of the Scottish Jacobites.

The front of the house, built in the seventeenth century, is pleasantly classical, without the severity of the later develop-

ment of that style, and is of fine masonry throughout. Other
parts are of a dark, irregular schist enlivened by coigns and
bands of white stone, very elegant and beautiful, with domed
roofs, surmounted by pillared cupolas, on the large round
corner towers.

The house is still occupied, and as is often the case with
houses of long habitation it contains a treasure of tapestries,
pictures, *objets d'art*, and antique furniture.

On the way back to Angers one should make a detour to visit
Béhuard, an antique village set on a rocky outcrop on a long
island in the Loire. Its houses are dark, with walls of the local
schist, in which a variety of freestones are used for doors and
windows, and many of them date from the fifteenth and sixteenth centuries. The church is distinguished by the favour of
Louis XI, who, after he had been rescued from drowning in the
Loire close to this island, made a vow of thanks to Our Lady of
Béhuard and showered the church with benefits, including
money for rebuilding. His interest was probably not altogether
as disinterested as it seems. Louis's nephew René was Duke of
Anjou and Louis was creating a base that might serve for the
easing of René out of his dukedom. In fact, René did leave
Anjou to spend the rest of his life in Provence, and in 1481
Louis annexed the duchy.

The church stands high and is reached by flights of steps. The
nave has a roof in the shape of an upturned boat, which one
may imagine, without seeking a basis in fact, to be an allusion to
Louis's contretemps in the Loire. There are fifteenth-century
fonts, sixteenth-century stalls with interesting misericords, and
chains given as ex-votos by freed prisoners brought back from
Algeria. A portrait of Louis XI given by Charles VIII in no way
flatters this ugliest of kings—the sly and wary eyes, the huge
nose, and the unbecoming headgear he affected, are rendered
without mercy. Béhuard was already a centre of pilgrimage
when Louis came here, and it has a venerated fifteenth-
century statue of the Virgin in a large crown and a great cloak,
like a stiffly costumed doll. The treasury of the church also

reflects Louis's generosity with a chalice, a processional cross, and a red velour cape woven with gold.

Thirteen kilometres north of Angers by the N162, we find the château of Plessis-Macé. Built in the twelfth century, fifty years before Saint-Louis rebuilt the château of Angers, Plessis-Macé served as an outlier, an advanced stronghold, to protect Angers against the Bretons. Strongly built and surrounded by moats, it presents today a first impression of the most picturesque of ruins, with a gable soaring above a wall on which the bold machicolations are obviously recent restorations. The general appearance of roofless ruin is misleading. You enter through an unimpressive gate into a vast, grassy courtyard bordered by low buildings of two storeys, with dormers breaking the slopes of steep slated roofs. The chapel is recognisable by its crocketed gable and flamboyant gothic window. The walls are of dark irregular schist and the details of doors and windows are all of new white stone. A great deal of restoration has been done on the exterior walls of Plessis-Macé. It includes a charming, heavily bracketed gothic balcony angled above an ogee-headed doorway in a corner, a balcony from which the ladies of the house might watch, from under the shelter of a jutting eave, the jousts or other entertainments or activities that went on in the courtyard (plate 35). Another such balcony opposite, on a wing that was the stables and the kitchen, was for the use of the servants, though it is scarcely less grand than the first. These buildings around the courtyard are roofed and intact and date from the fifteenth century. They were built up against the twelfth-century fortifications, as you may see inside by the depth of the embrasures of later windows cut in the massive outer walls. The interior rooms are large and spacious and are furnished with antique pieces of Spanish style, or, in one instance, in a Chinese style.

Plessis-Macé no longer impresses by its fortress strength. One leaves, rather, with a memory of rooms that, though large, might be comfortably domestic, except for the flamboyant gothic chapel, which has at the end opposite the altar an enormous wooden structure reaching far up to the roof, and providing an elevated private pew for the lord and his lady. Far, far above their heads, in the angle of the roof, servants and inferior members of the family might look steeply down from that uppermost level at the service of the mass, or, undiscovered, doze away the time.

To the north-east, beyond the Mayenne, stands another Plessis, Plessis-Bourré, the influence of which we have already encountered. Plessis-Bourré is the most delectable of gothic châteaux, its white walls doubly delectable as reflected in the still waters of its wide moats. The moats are wide because there is no rocky promontory here on which the château might be set. It stands on a plain now scattered with little woods, which was no doubt more thickly and more extensively wooden when Plessis-Bourré was built towards the end of the fifteenth century. Wide moats, fed from a stream, were essential for a fortress in this position, and the next best thing to unscaleable cliffs.

Jean Bourré, born in 1424, entered as a young man into the service of the Dauphin, who was a year older. Bourré served his master faithfully throughout his rebellious and difficult career, and was among the few men on whom the suspicious and usually untrusting Dauphin knew that he could rely. When the Dauphin became king as Louis XI in 1461 Bourré was not forgotten in the general apportionment of offices and awards that came with the new reign. He was given the lucrative posts of secretary of finance and treasurer of France.

Seven years later, in 1461, he began to build his new château on a site he had selected at a place called Plessis-le-Vent—a name suggestive of country over which in winter the winds blew cold and fresh. Langeais was already building under his supervision, and we can recognise at Plessis manifestly the same hand and the same mind. But Plessis is a much more attractive building than Langeais. Though it is certainly a fortified castle, even from the outside, where the fortifications are apparent, it has the air of being a house as much as a fortress. It was completed within five years, in a single build, and has a unity of design and purpose that was in its day uncommon. And it remains complete, with all four wings enclosing a square courtyard. A round tower, its roof *en poivrière*, stands at each corner. One of these towers is larger than the others and is obviously the keep or *donjon* (plate 34). It has the closely spaced machicolations, the covered wall-walk, and the set-back upper stage that we saw so well exemplified at Langeais, and which we also found at Ussé and at Brissac. All round the building the lower parts of the exterior walls and of the towers were originally blank, solid stone: there was to be no easy entry for an attacker. The windows of this ground storey seen today were not part of the original design—the rooms behind those walls were necessarily dim and dusky and as soon as it was thought safe to do so windows were made to let the light in.

Jean Bourré had a dislike of castle courtyards surrounded by tall buildings that kept out the air and the light, a dislike of the claustrophobic effect of enclosure. He therefore designed his new château to have wings of only two storeys, except for the *logis*, that is the wing in which he was to live; this he made three storeys high, so that it overlooked the other wings and enjoyed views far over the countryside. This single innovation influenced the building of several other châteaux, notably Le Verger and Bury, both of which, however, have been destroyed. From what one may judge of Langeais, this may not have been the pattern there.

The château is entered over a bridge across the moat, a bridge that ended at a drawbridge in front of the gatehouse, where the vertical slots for the arms that raised it are still to be seen. To the left of this gatehouse a flèche on the roof announces the chapel. The courtyard is more patently domestic in its buildings and its windows, and in fact the château is still lived in. Because of this we were forbidden to take photographs anywhere within the courtyard or in the rooms shown to visitors.

Despite its inhabitation, a large part of the château is shown. On one side of the courtyard an open arcaded gallery after the fashion of Charles d'Orléans at Blois contains a collection of antique horse carriages. Inside, the chapel of Saint-Anne is shown, and the justice room, and other rooms furnished with interesting pieces, including an excellent collection of fans. There are some good chimney-pieces. But perhaps what the visitor remembers best is the fifteenth-century coffered ceiling of the guard-room on the first floor, every coffer of which—and I have forgotten how many of them there are—is filled with an allegorical, a humorous, or a rude little picture, some of them frank enough to make a Sunday-school teacher blush. One shows a wolf-like creature with cavernous sides and every rib protruding. This is Chicheface, whose delicate stomach can prosper only on a diet of chaste women—which is why the animal is so obviously starving.

Our guide here, dressed in clothes like a gardener's, with a flat cap on his head, seemed at first sight inauspicious, a man subtracted from his main occupation merely to fill in for an unwelcome chore. This impression was quite wrong. He turned out to be by far the best château guide we had encountered anywhere along the Loire valley. He had a vast amount of information in his head (I hope it was correct) and he imparted it with an enthusiasm in no way diminished by his having to do it several times a day. He asked me if I could tell where he came from, but my French is not such that I could emulate in that language the feats of Bernard Shaw's Professor Higgins in English. I knew he came from somewhere to the north—he was in fact Belgian—but he had been in the Loire valley since the war. As there were several English people in our party he offered to speak (in French) more slowly than usual, and then his enthusiasm got the better of him and he rattled on at top speed, while I, floundering after, translated for a young couple who knew no French—searching while in the guard-room for words that would not offend their plainly susceptible feelings.

Châteaux stand for centuries, but guides come and go. You may not find our Belgian there, but I hope that you will.

Montgeoffroy, twenty-four kilometres east of Angers by the D61, is one of the latest in date of the châteaux we have examined along the Loire valley. It was built from 1775 in a handsome classical style, but the name it bears is that of a man who founded a château here in the thirteenth century— Geoffroi de Châteaubriant. His château was rebuilt in the sixteenth century, except for two squat round towers with conical roofs, which remain, forming terminals to the wings of the present château. The chapel is also of this period.

In 1676 the château passed into the hands of the Contades family, who have held it ever since. It was a member of this family, a marshal of France, who rebuilt the château in its present form. He went to Paris for his architect, Nicolas Barre, and from Paris came his decorators and furnishers.

The eighteenth-century part of the château, that is to say the house itself, is strictly symmetrical and as is the case with other buildings of this time it seems to have been designed to be seen only from directly in front. As at Cheverny, built more than a hundred years earlier but just as symmetrical, the drive runs straight as a ruler for the entrance door, thus imposing on visitors that central, symmetrical view. Photographers and painters evidently feel strongly the compulsion to stand in the middle of the drive, or to take their stance outside the ornate entrance gates in order to centre the château within the wrought iron.

The house is of three storeys, with a pedimented centre-piece of three bays and narrow, projecting wings at the sides. There is no attempt at fortification—by this time the notion of a château as a castle had been forgotten, and not even the two low sixteenth-century towers could be supposed to have been retained for the seigneurial effect of a *donjon*. The chapel and the stable wing and the two towers form the limits of a raised terrace deep in gravel and divided from what is now meadow by a balustrade.

The interior is what one comes to Montgeoffroy to see. The house is still inhabited and is fully furnished. The interest of the furniture, apart from its quality and its period, is that it is almost all of it the furniture that was bought for the house when it was completed. An inventory made in 1780 is applicable for the greater part to the present day. As the furniture, the paintings, and the décor of the rooms in which they are set are in excellent condition, one has the experience of walking through a house of another epoch, in which one might at any moment encounter the Maréchal de Contades or one of his family, coming to welcome you or to inquire what you had come for, and what you are doing in their house.

The stable block contains a tack-room that will arouse the envy of riding enthusiasts. Whips, saddles, straps, horse-collars, bits, and bridles hang on the walls, amid an odour of polished leather.

The sixteenth-century chapel is small, with scarcely sufficient space for the owner and his lady and all the numerous band of retainers such a house and such an estate would have had. But the quality of the building is not skimped. You enter through a gothic doorway into a late-gothic interior, rising to a roof elaborately ribbed, with bosses painted and gilt at the intersections, a late example of an Angevin vault. The window over the altar is filled with sixteenth-century glass showing a series of scenes from the Bible. The lower right-hand panel is different. It shows a man in a short surcoat, kneeling with his hands in prayer. It is probably meant to represent Guillaume de la Grandière, the builder of the château of which only this chapel and the two towers remain.

12. The Valley of the Loir

The valley of the Loir, that river so confusingly named and to be distinguished from the feminine Loire (with an e), makes an interesting route homewards for the visitor almost satiated with châteaux and monasteries. This is a way back to Paris or to one of the channel ports. Châteaux do not punctuate the route as frequently as in the Loire valley and it cannot be claimed that those you will see are of major interest.

Coming from Angers we pass at a kilometre or so the château of Le Verger. There is little point in visiting it, for even if you could get in there is not a great deal to see. Yet there was here a very large château indeed, built in the late fifteenth century by Pierre de Rohan-Guéminée, who is said to have saved the life of Charles VIII when the convoy of mules that brought the Renaissance to France was attacked at Fornova. He had thereafter the favour of the king and held high office in the king's service. His château owed elements of its design to Jean Bourré and Plessis-Bourré, as may be seen in engravings made when the château was still complete. A later owner, the Cardinal de Rohan, sold the château to a rich merchant. The merchant one day boasted that the bones of his family would lie in the chapel with those of the Rohans. This remark was reported to the cardinal, who promptly exercised a legal right to buy the château back. He then ordered its demolition. All that remains now is a *châtelet*, flint towers, and the kitchens.

The main road goes on to Durtal, parallel with but at some distance from the Loir. At Durtal the road crosses the river by a bridge and your eye is immediately caught by the high walls of a château that positively leaps into the air from the street along which the village is strung. The first impression is of military strength and that was what was intended when the château was built in the fifteenth century; but it is of two periods, as you may see when you have recovered from your surprise. The round towers, with machicolations and pepperpot roofs, which confer a forceful character on the outline of the building, are of the fifteenth century. The residential part, with rectangular windows and shaped dormers, belongs to the next century. The builder of the earlier part was François de Scépeaux, Maréchal de Vieilleville, and here he entertained Henri II, Charles IX, and Catherine de Médicis. The building was damaged at the Revolution and subsequently altered.

The apparently inaccessible château one sees from the bridge is in fact easily accessible from the other side. Visitors may go into the courtyard and even climb to the battlements, but you may be, as we were, watched with fascinated and uncomfortable attention by one of the inmates, for the place is now a *maison de retraite*.

From Durtal we go by the D18 through Montigny-les-Rairies and Cheviré-le-Rouge to Baugé, where Yolande of Aragon and her son René of Anjou had one of their favourite châteaux. This château, originally built by Foulques Nerra in the tenth century, was rebuilt by René in a style that is reminiscent of a castle in Scotland. Yolande employed Scottish mercenaries to fight in a battle at the neighbouring Vieille-Baugé against the English. Is it possible that among them were masons from Scotland who were employed on the erection of the château— on one of the turrets there are little figures of masons at their work. Whether or no the masons were Scots, it is amusing to see that the connection with Scotland is maintained: Baugé is twinned with Milngavie.

The château stands in the middle of a vast, arid, open space that was once occupied by walls and moats. There is ample space for parking, and a regimented grove of trees to give shelter from the sun. The building is put to practical use. It contains the Hôtel de Ville, the Syndicat d'Intiatives, and a museum that exhibits collections of coins, of weapons, and of faience.

The château of Baugé has a spiral staircase in the gothic manner, but this one is distinguished, as is that at Montreuil-Bellay, by the shallowness and the width of its steps. It ascends to a vault in which the central pillar sprouts ribs as a palm tree sprouts branches, with a variety of carved bosses.

The chapel of the Filles du Cœur de Marie in a narrow street in the town belonged to an eighteenth-century hospice. You may push open the door, and find yourself, as we did, in the middle of a service. For adoration goes on continually in this chapel. The reason is that there is here a piece of the True Cross, or at least a piece of wood with that reputation that was brought from the Holy Land in the year 1241. In the fifteenth century it was carved into the shape of a double-armed cross, the kind of cross that became well known during the Hitler war as the cross of Lorraine. Indeed it was from this cross of Baugé, this cross of Anjou, that René II, Duke of Lorraine, derived the symbol he put on his flag in the fifteenth century. The wooden cross was originally given to the Cistercian monastery of La Boissière about eighteen kilometres to the east of Baugé, where the former abbey has been transformed into a château. The cross was brought to Baugé in 1790. With a figure of Christ carved on each side and enriched with gold and jewels, this precious relic brings a constant stream of the faithful to the chapel of the Filles du Cœur de Marie.

East of Baugé, on the road to Pontigné, a good example of a dolmen stands in a wood about a kilometre from the road. The lane to it is narrow and not good for vehicles; it makes a pleasant green walk. The dolmen has a huge capstone and is prefaced by a kind of porch also with a capstone.

The village of Pontigné is old, with tumbledown houses, in the midst of which is an impressive church. The doorway was once magnificent, but is now very worn. The spire is distinctly

spiral in the Anjou fashion. The interior of the church has some
interest, despite a pretentious classical altar piece. Some good
wall paintings decorate an alcove, and there are carved capitals
that retain traces of their original colour.

A minor road to the north leads to the N817 and in about
twenty kilometres to Le Lude, where the N159 descends
through narrow streets to a bridge over the Loir. The château,
built on a bluff above the river, is set tightly up against the road
on one side, while on the others it dominates an attractive
garden and beyond the river a green and leafy landscape. The
garden, which you may enter for a separate fee at times when
the house itself is not open, is ornamented with eighteenth-
century stone vases on pedestals, and has a long balustrade the
length of the cliff edge, above the river.

Architecturally, Le Lude is a box of all-sorts. There was a
château here in the middle ages, which for a brief eight years
up to 1427 was in the hands of the English. Twenty years later
it came into the possession of the Daillon family, who proceeded
to rebuild it. The work was intermittent and protracted. One
of the reasons for this was that Jean de Daillon quitted the
service of the rebellious Dauphin for that of the king, Charles
VII. Whereas Jean Bourré served the Dauphin faithfully and
was rewarded with high office when the Dauphin became king
as Louis XI, Jean de Daillon had to take refuge in a cave, where
he remained for seven years. He was eventually forgiven,
however, and became chamberlain to the king and governor
of the Dauphiné. The difference in these two careers is mirrored
in the châteaux. Plessis-Bourré, built *d'un seul jet*, is all of a
piece; Le Lude, built over centuries, is all of pieces. There are
four great, fat, corner towers at Le Lude, with machicolations
and covered wall-walks, that look as though they belong to a
military château. Joining them are three wings, all of different
periods and styles, with the fourth side closed by a triple-arched
screen. The left wing is of the time of Louis XII. The right wing,
overlooking the terrace garden, belongs to the period of
François I, and in its ornate pilasters and its spired and

decorative dormers, you may recognise inspiration from François's work at Blois. The fourth side, looking down on to the river, is of the time of Louis XVI, a classical façade with a frontispiece of three bays surmounted by a pediment.

The house is furnished and occupied and you see an interesting series of rooms in the three wings, including in the François I wing a splendid library hung with Gobelin tapestries.

The master mason of the château begun in 1479 was Jean Gendrot. A house was built for him just outside the château gate, and it is still there, typical of its period and distinct from anything else in the village. A street, the Rue Gendrottière, also commemorates him.

We now take a long drive, twenty-one kilometres through Château-du-Loir, where the Yre joins the Loir, and thirteen kilometres farther to La Chartre-sur-le-Loir. About six kilometres beyond this we come to the château of Poncé beside the road. But pause first in the village, to go into the church. It has some remarkable twelfth-century frescoes.

Poncé is a not very large château of the sixteenth century, and it is not well known—no doubt because it is a little aside from the common tourist routes. Yet it is full of interest. The first thing you will remark is the extraordinary garden. The château rests at the foot of a cliff, and the cliff face has been turned into a curious feature, with a path wandering up it, past caves dug into the *tuffeau*. At the top and high in the air a nineteenth-century owner constructed a fanciful wall of bright red brick or terra-cotta. What were the stables now contain a museum of local crafts, in which a miscellany of bygones is crowded as fascinatingly as in an antique shop. Another part of the château contains an active pottery, which you may visit to see pots of many kinds being made by the wheel or by hand, coloured, and fired; and you may buy them in a showroom.

Finally, the house itself. We walked round without a guide, under our own steam, as it were. The building is tall and there are many stairs to climb—but what stairs! The staircase of Poncé at least has a reputation, rating two stars in Michelin.

The flights are straight, parallel one with the other, and they climb under ceilings of white stone carved into coffers, each of which is finely sculptured with little scenes or portraits. The staircase alone makes a visit to Poncé worth while, but there is so much else to see, so many odds and ends, including a pigeon-house for eighteen hundred birds, complete with its turning ladder or *potence*, that you should allow most of a morning or an afternoon to see it.

Pierre Ronsard, the poet and prior of Saint-Côme, was born in 1524 at the manor of the Possonière a few kilometres to the south-east of Poncé. The poet's father, Louis de Ronsard, was in Italy at the beginning of the sixteenth century and, just as Charles VIII did, he came back with his head full of the charm and the ideas of Italy. He put them into effect by altering his house, a simple manor with an octagonal stair-case tower, into the renaissance style, with a variety of inscriptions carved in Latin and French. Pierre de Ronsard spent his boyhood here and as a grown man was often at the house.

The name is properly 'la Possonière', from a word meaning a measure; but the Ronsard arms include three fishes, and from this fact has come the name la Poissonnière. Both versions, with and without the i, are still current.

We follow the N817 up the valley of the Loir to Troo. The name 'Troo' seems humorous, suggests something odd, and in a sense this is apposite, for Troo is a notable home of troglodytes. A high cliff of *tuffeau* is carved out like gruyère cheese on various levels from the base to the top, and in these holes people live in a style that may be called uncomfortable only because of the stiff climb that has to be undertaken to reach their front doors. Their 'streets' are ledges, which are connected one with another by flights of stairs. The troglodytes of Troo must develop sturdy calves from constant climbing. Some of these houses open their doors to visitors and for a fee for which you might see a château you may look into a caveman's dwelling.

The cliff is cut and tunnelled more than you may suppose.

There are labyrinths of passages cut deep into the earth, originally as refuges during the upheaval and dangers of many wars.

A breathless, toiling climb up the hill leads to the collegiate church of Saint-Martin, built as a romanesque church in the eleventh century and altered in the twelfth to the Angevin style. The vaults inside are of the 'parasol' type we have seen already in Angers and elsewhere, but we are now back in the Orléanais, as we have been since La Chartre-sur-le-Loir.

On the main road, in the valley, stands the Maladrerie Saint-Catherine, a romanesque rest-house built for the benefit of sick and leprous pilgrims passing on their long journey to Saint James of Compostela. The pilgrims may have passed on to the far side of the river to visit the modest little church of Saint-Jacques-de-Guérets, and look at Byzantinesque murals of the life and passion of Christ painted about the middle of the twelfth century.

There are more very fine murals of the twelfth and thirteenth centuries seven kilometres distant at the next town of Montoire, where the Loir flows clear and clean and anglers take advantage of fish in waters sheltered by weeping willows. You may park— if it is not market day—in a large tree-bordered *place* in the middle of the town, the Place Clémenceau. From here a short walk down the Rue Ronsard brings you to the bridge over the river. It is the 'Rue Ronsard' because Pierre Ronsard was titular head of the priory of Saint-Gilles on the south side of the river—he was here for the last time in 1585, two months before he died at Saint-Côme near Tours. As you walk along the street you have in front of you a large hill, on the summit of which stands a ruined square keep of the eleventh century. If you take the trouble to collect the key from a café on the Lavardin road you may visit the château, the principal merit of which is not the ruin itself but the view over the valley of the Loir and of the neighbouring château of Lavardin, also on a hill.

But pause on the bridge over the Loir for the benefit of the pleasant view up and down the river. The street that continues it on the south side is the Rue Oustrille. An attractive renaissance house stands on the right-hand side of this street, on the corner of an alley. Opposite is a miscellaneous little shop dignified by the title of *droguerie*, and here you may obtain the key of the chapel of Saint-Gilles. This is what we did, and crossed the road to enter the alley beside the renaissance house, when a young man came running after us. His mother had told him that we were here and he was, he said, the official guide for the chapel of Saint-Gilles. He was an amiable person, but I could not help thinking that if all the official and unofficial guides in France could be sent to the moon, I for one would not be sorry.

The eleventh-century chapel of Saint-Gilles, itself little more than the sanctuary of the original chapel, is all that remains of the priory founded in the seventh century, which in its day was known to the pilgrims travelling to Tours on the road to Compostela. Montoire, as did Troo, had its *maladrerie* for sick pilgrims. The pilgrims would come into the chapel of Saint-Gilles and admire the murals, as we can admire them today, for they are for the most part in very good condition. There are several figures of Christ of the twelfth century, and another of the thirteenth, painted on the curved surfaces of the vaults of the apses and showing unmistakably the influence of the art of Byzantium. The figures look down peacefully, benignly, and with round eyes, perhaps a little puzzled, on the gawping visitors of the twentieth century. It is, in fact, when looking at things above your head, difficult not to gawp.

Montoire was the scene of a meeting on the 22nd of October 1940, after the fall of France, between Hitler and Pierre Laval, and the following day between Hitler and Marshal Pétain. Hitler hoped to persuade them to bring France into the war against England. The town had never before seen such precautions as were put into effect at this time to ensure Hitler's safety. The place was taken over entirely by German forces, who kept the Montoiriens in their houses and cut off all connection with the outside world. Why was Montoire chosen for these interviews? Among the reasons was undoubtedly the fact that the town was on a railway line, with a tunnel. Hitler's headquarters were in a railway carriage, and if the R.A.F. interfered the train could have been drawn into the tunnel without delay.

The valley of the Loir continues up to Vendôme, and then up to Châteaudun and towards Chartres. But this is out of our province, and here we close this book.

Appendix

Visiting the châteaux

Anyone planning an extended tour of the châteaux of the Loire valley would be wise to take into account the cost of entry fees. It is not a minor item. A family of four may find that they will have to pay the equivalent of four pounds for each of the better-known châteaux, and not a great deal less for others. What you get for your money is another matter. If you go in the height of the season and are herded round with little chance to see anything, you may well feel that you are not getting your money's worth. Or you may believe, as I did at Cheverny, that not enough is shown anyway to warrant the cost.

In general the châteaux owned by the state are the better bargains—these include Blois, Chambord, Chinon, Loches, Langeais, Chenonceau, Azay-le-Rideau—but they are not the only 'best buys'. I would include Plessis-Bourré and Fougères-sur-Bièvre near the top of the list. My 'worst buys' are Cheverny and Saumur.

Amateurs of the arts, of sculpture, painting, furniture, décor, and all the other details that bring a house alive, will not find much satisfaction in the châteaux of the Loire, despite the fact that many châteaux are brimful of treasures of these kinds. The guide system simply does not allow sufficient time for study or appreciation of anything. I recall only three exceptions—Chambord, Chenonceau, and Angers—the latter only for the tapestry of the Apocalypse—where you may go around at your own pace.

Photography is allowed in nearly all the châteaux mentioned in this book except Plessis-Bourré. In many instances there is an extra charge, which I noticed a number of people ignored. Flash is forbidden in some places, tripods practically everywhere, unless you pay extra yet again. One place proposed to claim extra for colour film, but how that could possibly be enforced I could not say.

Travel

Perhaps the pleasantest way to travel in the Loire valley would be by bicycle—the speed slow enough for the countryside and the riverscape to be enjoyed and fast enough to cover fifteen or twenty miles between one château and another in not too great a time; but you would need a long stay in France if you wished to see more than a small number of châteaux. Alternatively there are package tours, but there are none of these that I have found that do more than visit a small number of the more famous châteaux, or decant you in Tours or Blois and then leave you to yourself. Most people who set out to explore the valley will without doubt go by car. Although some of the major roads of France, constantly chewed up by huge lorries, have atrocious surfaces on which driving for the ordinary motorist is painful, the roads of the Loire valley in the region covered by this book are uniformly excellent, whether of the D (*départementale*) class or the more important N (*nationale*) class. The tourist in the Loire valley will come upon roads marked Vo on Michelin pillars; these *voisinage* roads may be narrow, but for the most part the surface is satisfactory.

Hotels

The Loire valley is a tourist area and there are consequently many hotels of various grades. French hotels are classified for quality and facilities and information and prices may be found in the three guide-books following:

The Michelin Guide (the 'Red Book')
Guide to the Logis de France and Auberges de France
Guide des Relais Routiers.

What you may consider a good hotel depends on what you expect from an hotel, and what you expect to pay. The three guides quoted represent, in general terms, hotels in descending order of cost—the hotels in Michelin mostly cost more than do the *logis* and *auberges*, and the *logis* and *auberges* are more costly than the *Routiers*.

If you want sitting-rooms, writing-rooms, television, and such facilities, then you must pay a higher price and you will find your hotel in Michelin. At the other end of the scale, the *Routiers* are primarily for lorry-drivers (though they will take tourists willingly), and their prices are appropriate. I have little experience of *Routier* hotels, and have not had much luck with those I have tried, but other people have reported well of them. You can expect to find a comfortable bedroom with hot and cold water and probably a bidet, and meals large enough to satisfy a hungry man. But it would be optimistic to look for the best quality of cooking or of food in every *Routier*.

The *logis* and the *auberges* maintain a higher standard, and it is among these that I look first when I am in France. In a *logis* you may have a comfortable bedroom with h. and c., bidet, shower, and sometimes a w.c., in an hotel with a good restaurant and probably a bar.

Some people complain that France is an expensive country for the tourist, and in some respects it is. The restaurants of the *logis*, however, are by no means expensive. You may have a full-course table-d'hôte meal, with a choice of alternative dishes, for a price not much more than half of what you would have to pay in England for a meal of similar quality, if you could find it. What *is* expensive in France is a snack of any kind.

One of the curiosities of French country hotels is that they close for a day during the week and in some instances for a whole fortnight or even a month in the summer. Some hotels close down for the whole of the winter. Restaurants may close one day a week. Consult the appropriate guide-book for these closures.

The disadvantage of the *logis* is that they are for the most part in villages or in the country, and may not be convenient for the exploration of towns such as Orléans, Tours, or Angers.

My wife and I had no disappointments by choosing *logis* haphazardly. On the contrary, we had the good fortune to find a series of them with restaurants progressively better as we moved down the valley.

We recommend the following hotels:

Châteauneuf-sur-Loire. La Capitainerie, Hostellerie du Parc, is one of the more expensive *logis*, but it is pleasant and comfortable, with a good restaurant. Good situation next to the park and near the town centre.

Chitenay, about six kilometres west of Cheverny and ten south of Blois. A convenient place for a number of châteaux, but itself a village of little interest. *La Clé des Champs* is a little old-fashioned but it has a good restaurant.

Luynes. The Hôtel de la Halle is slightly primitive in its accommodation, but M. and Madame Neveu are cheerful and welcoming and their restaurant is interesting and worth trying.

Chacé, south of Saumur. *The Auberge de Thouet* was rebuilt in 1972 and is now a comfortable hotel. I would classify the restaurant as moderately good.

Saint-Sylvain d'Anjou, about six kilometres north-east of Angers. Somewhat out of the way, but the *Auberge d'Éventard* is worth seeking out—it is not in the village but some distance off on the main road. The restaurant is the best we found anywhere in the Loire valley at anything like the price, and because it is so it is wise, if you are not staying there, to book your table. The menu is long and varied, the cheese trolley a conspectus of French cheeses. You could make a meal out of a first course of *crudités*, and if you do not resist temptation you will have no space left for what follows. It is inexplicable to me that this restaurant is graded with only one star NN (Nouvelles Normes). It will undoubtedly be upgraded and will then cost more.

Wine

Though I have drunk quantities of different kinds of wine, and have read much about wine, I make not the slightest pretence to the title of connoisseur. Certainly I am not a gourmet. I do not possess the palate to distinguish nuances of difference and quality, and in that I have no doubt I resemble many of the readers of this book. On the other hand I have small respect for and give little credit to many of those who write so learnedly and so eclectically or esoterically about wine; if they had half the experience they suggest they have they would be in a permanent state of inebriation.

In order to evaluate and compare wines one must have special sensory qualities, not only a precise and perceptive palate, but also a precise memory for taste and bouquet; I believe this latter quality to be extremely rare. However, this does not mean that for those of us with duller perception there is no pleasure in drinking wine. Indeed there is. And there is pleasure in its many other qualities, its bouquet, its colour, its texture, and above all in what it can confer upon the flavour and enjoyment of a meal. For though wine may be enjoyed for its own sake, it is when it is drunk with a meal that it is most pleasurable.

The wines of the Loire are many and varied. Most of them are light, and most of them are slightly sweet, and most of them are white or rosé; but all of these statements are qualified because there are notable Loire wines that do not correspond to them. There are little local wines, that is to say wines made in such small quantities that they may be bought only in the neighbourhood of the vineyard and may be exhausted before the end of the year after that in which the grapes were picked. These are wines that are drunk when they are new, as many Loire wines may be. There are others, such as Vouvray, that are known throughout the world and which may be stored for years, improving all the time.

The colour is variable too. There are white wines that are colourless, or even 'grey', there are others that are yellow verging towards green, as Sancerre and Vouvray. Some rosés are so light in colour that they might be called pinkish white, some so dark that they verge towards red. Reds may tend towards rosé on the one hand or on the other towards a dark purplish red, as Bourgueil, which is so dark it is almost opaque. But of nearly all Loire wines you may recognise one salient characteristic—the taste is fresh and clean.

The better-class wines are sold in bottles marked on the label *Appellation contrôlée*. A second class is marked *Vin délimité de Qualité supérieure* or 'V.D.Q.S.' These are official classifications.

This is not the place for a discussion in depth of the quality and variety of wine. It is sufficient to remark that the best wines are grown on soil that would be regarded as poor or barren for other kinds of agriculture. Rich clay makes a wine perhaps high in alcohol but probably lacking subtlety. Much of the country along the Loire is based on the white limestone called *tuffeau*, and this is ideal land for the vine. There is also, lower downstream and near Angers, a soil of shaly schist and sand, which produces some very fine wine.

We may follow the river downstream for a superficial survey.

We begin with Sancerre and Pouilly-sur-Loire on opposing sides of the river. These two areas make somewhat similar wines of a yellow-green colour, slightly sweet, and said to have a taste of gun-flints—a comment that means little to anybody not in the habit of chewing gun-flints. Sancerre and Pouilly-Fumé are made from the Sauvignon grape, Pouilly-sur-Loire from the Chasselas. Each of these three wines is an excellent accompaniment for fish, for salads, and other light meals.

In the district of Orléans a number of minor red wines are produced, but not exported elsewhere. Cour-Cheverny, the village near the château of Cheverny, makes a white wine from the Romarantin grape, a grape you will not meet again along the Loire.

Vouvray and Montlouis, facing each other across the Loire, produce similar white wines of considerable reputation, from the Chenin blanc grape. These are wines that live long in the bottle and improve for many years. Vouvray has the better quality of the two. Vouvray and Montlouis are slightly frizzy. A distinctly sparkling wine is also made, the better qualities by the champagne method.

The villages of Bourgueil, Saint-Nicolas-de-Bourgueil, and the town of Chinon are the centres of a red wine area. Bourgueil may be very dark in colour and is an excellent wine for red meat or any strongly flavoured dish. The red wine of Chinon is softer. The grape is the Cabernet franc.

Anjou makes excellent white wines, a few good red wines, and some of the best rosé wines in France. The rosé wines are made throughout the province, from Cabernet, Gamay, and Cot grapes. The wine is dry or slightly sweet, the colour variable. The red comes from the Cabernet, Pineau d'Aunis, and Gamay grapes, some of which are grown in the neighbourhood of Saumur. The white wines come mostly from the Chenin grape, and some from vineyards small in acreage but high in quality. Such is the Coulée de Serrant, near the château of Serrant. Quarts de Chaume (which is so named from a former custom of surrendering a quarter of the product to the seigneur), Bonnezeau, and Savennières, all on shaly land, produce the three best white wines of Anjou, each with its *appellation contrôlée*. Bonnezeau and Quarts de Chaume are made from grapes affected by the 'noble rot'. This is a fungus, *Botrytis cinerea*, that has the effect of reducing the moisture in the grape and concentrating the sugar in it. At the *vendange* the grapes are not picked by the bunch, but are selected in two or three pickings as they are ready.

White wines of good quality are made also in the region of Saumur and along the Côteaux du Layon.

There are more vineyards downstream to the Nantais region, where the famous Muscadet comes from, but these are outside the scope of this book.

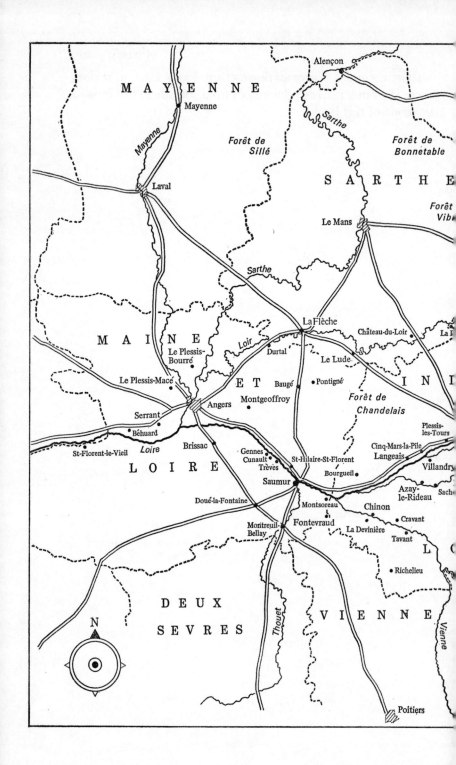

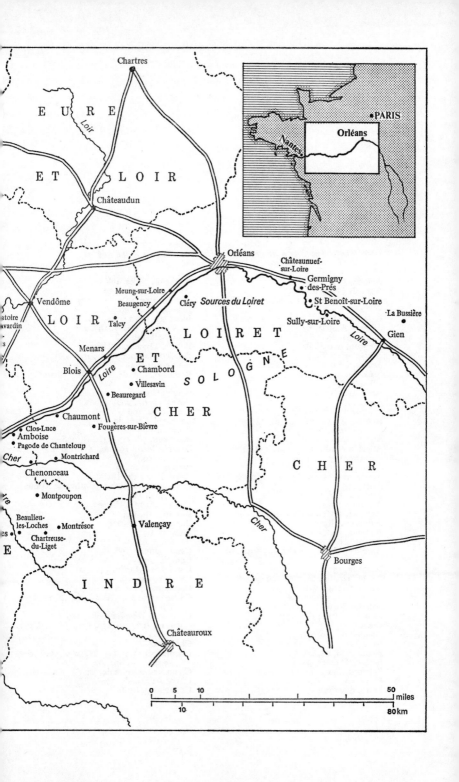

Index